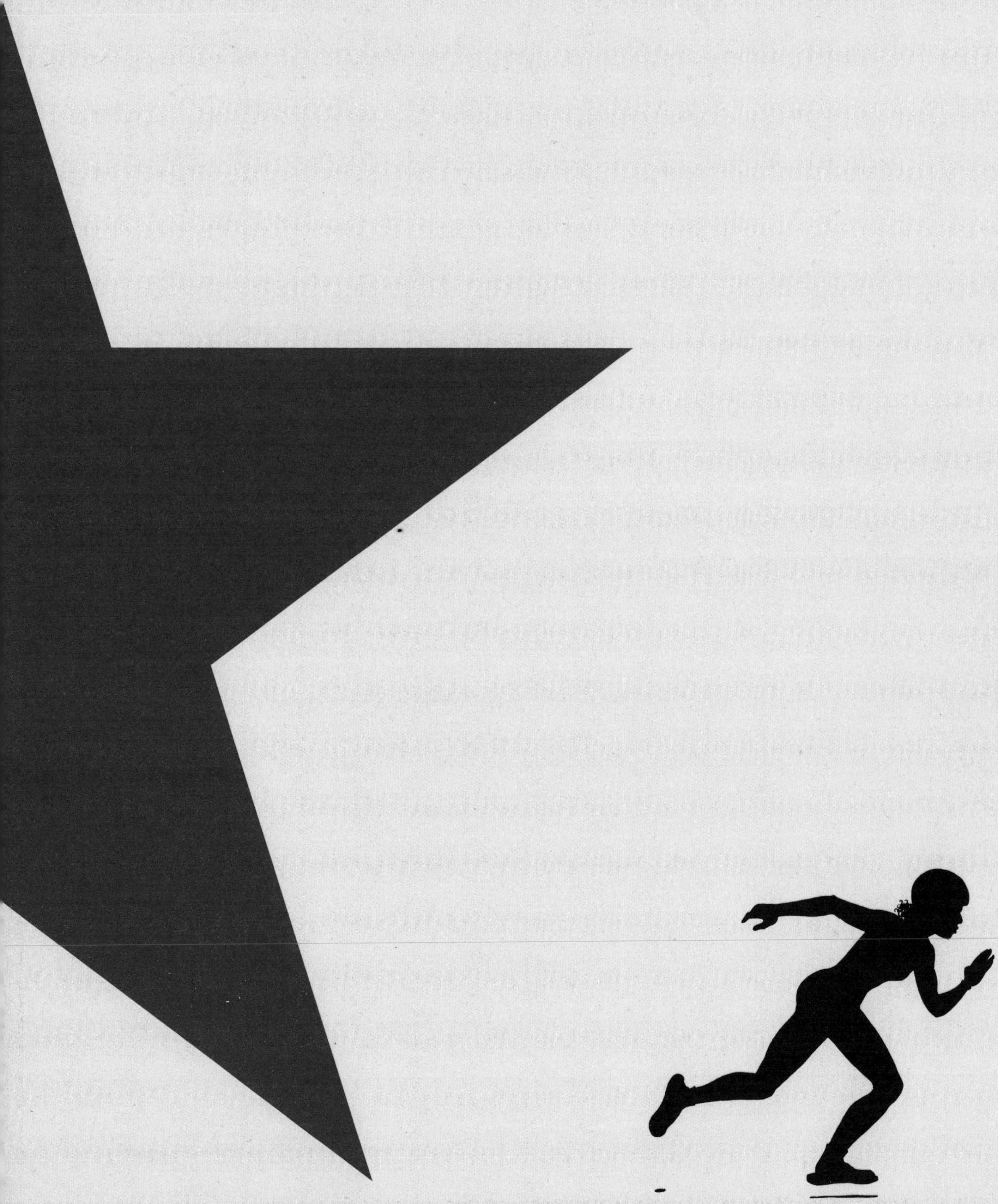

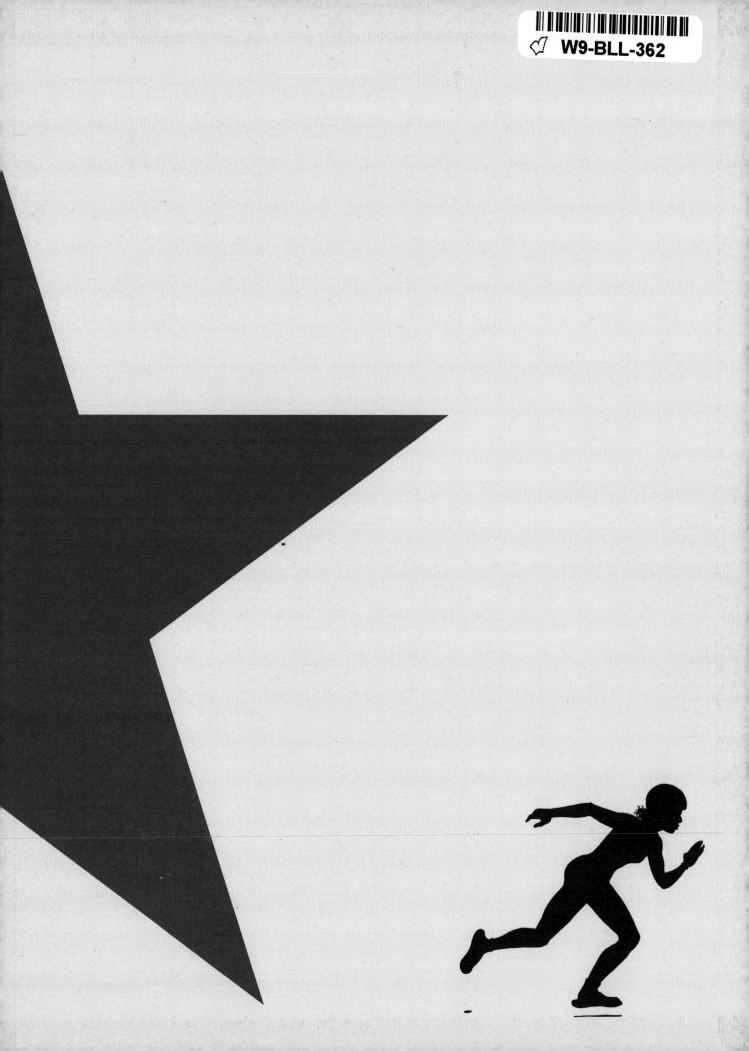

JESSICA ABEL

TRISH TRASH

❶
❷
❸

TRASH

ROLLERGIRL OF MARS

By Jessica Abel

Background and Design
Lydia Roberts

Colors
Walter

SUPER
GENIUS

New York

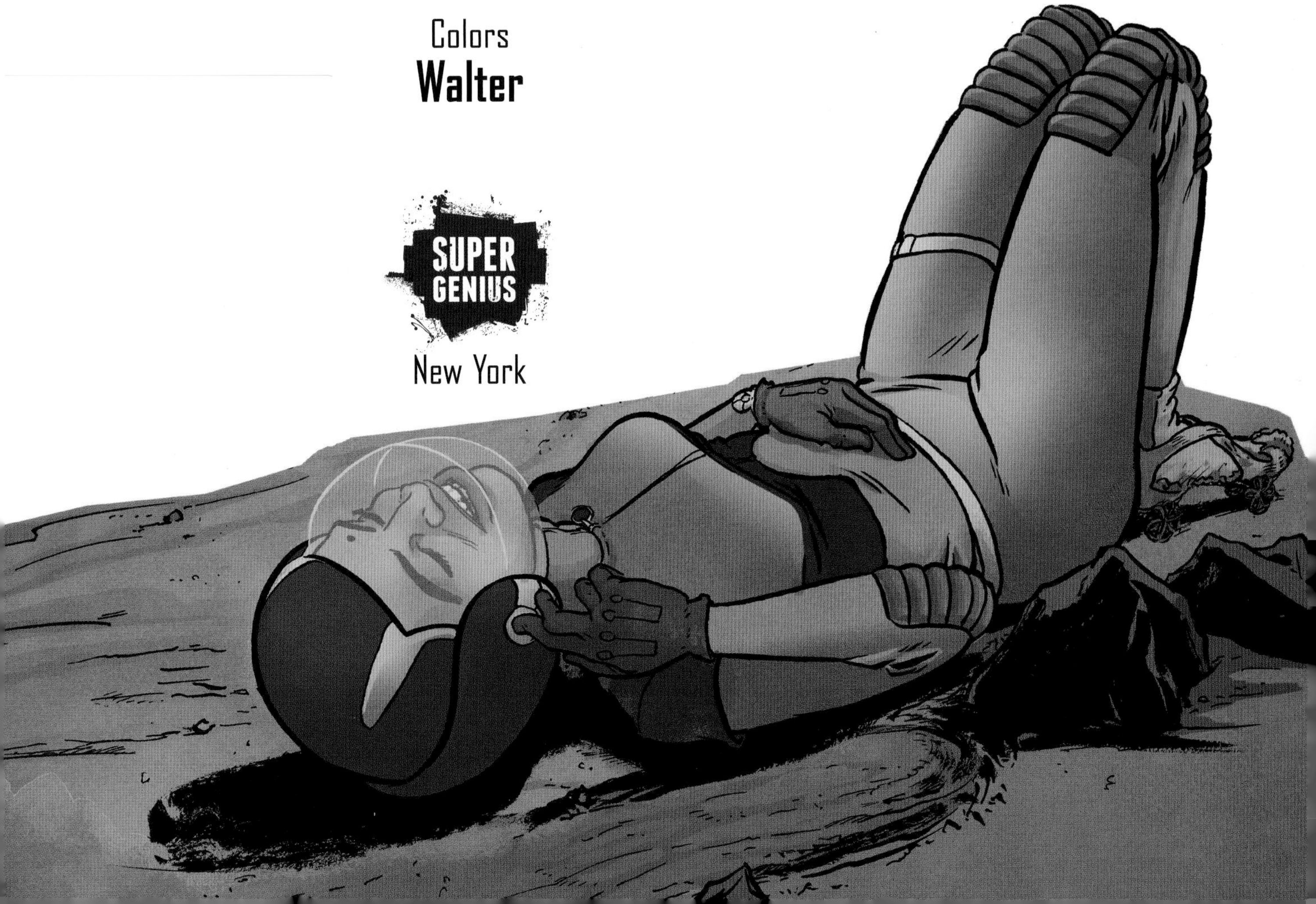

JESSICA ABEL
TRISH TRASH
❶
❷
❸
ROLLERGIRL OF MARS

Backgrounds and design by Lydia Roberts
Colors by Walter
Wikimarz.red art and colors by Lydia Roberts

Super Genius books may be purchased for business or promotional use. For information on bulk purchases please contact Macmillan Corporate and Premium Sales Department at (800) 221-7945 x 5442

Super Genius graphic novels are also available digitally wherever e-books are sold.

Super Genius is an imprint of Papercutz.

Dawn Guzzo – Production Coordinator
Jeff Whitman – Editor
Jim Salicrup
Editor-in-Chief

ISBN: 978-1-62991-639-2

Printed in China
August 2017

Distributed by Macmillan
First Super Genius Printing

Our Story So Far...

Seven-and-a-half-year-old (that's fifteen in Earth years), Patricia "Trish Trash" Nupindju is a talented young hoverderby player on Mars 200 years in the future. Trish wants desperately to go pro with her local team, the Terror Novas, because it seems like the only way to escape a future of poverty and hard labor on her aunt and uncle's moisture farm in Candor Chasma, where they work as indentured labor for the Arex Corporation.

But she's too young to get a contract, so Trish takes an unpaid intern contract to become the team's equipment-handler, their "skategirl," instead of skating. Seemed like a good idea at the time, but the loss of her labor pushes her family's farm even closer to the brink.

When she encounters an indigenous Martian "bug" out in the rough near her farmhouse, it puts everything into question. Could this Martian change Trish's fate? And why won't her best friend Marq return her calls?

TRISH TRASH # 1   TRISH TRASH # 2

TRISH TRASH graphic novels are available at booksellers everywhere in hardcover only for $14.99 each. Or order from us—please add $4.00 for postage and handling for the first book, add $1.00 for each additional book. Please make check payable to NBM Publishing.
Send to: SUPER GENIUS, 160 Broadway, Suite 700, East Wing, New York, NY 10038 (1-800-886-1223)
www.supergeniuscomics.com

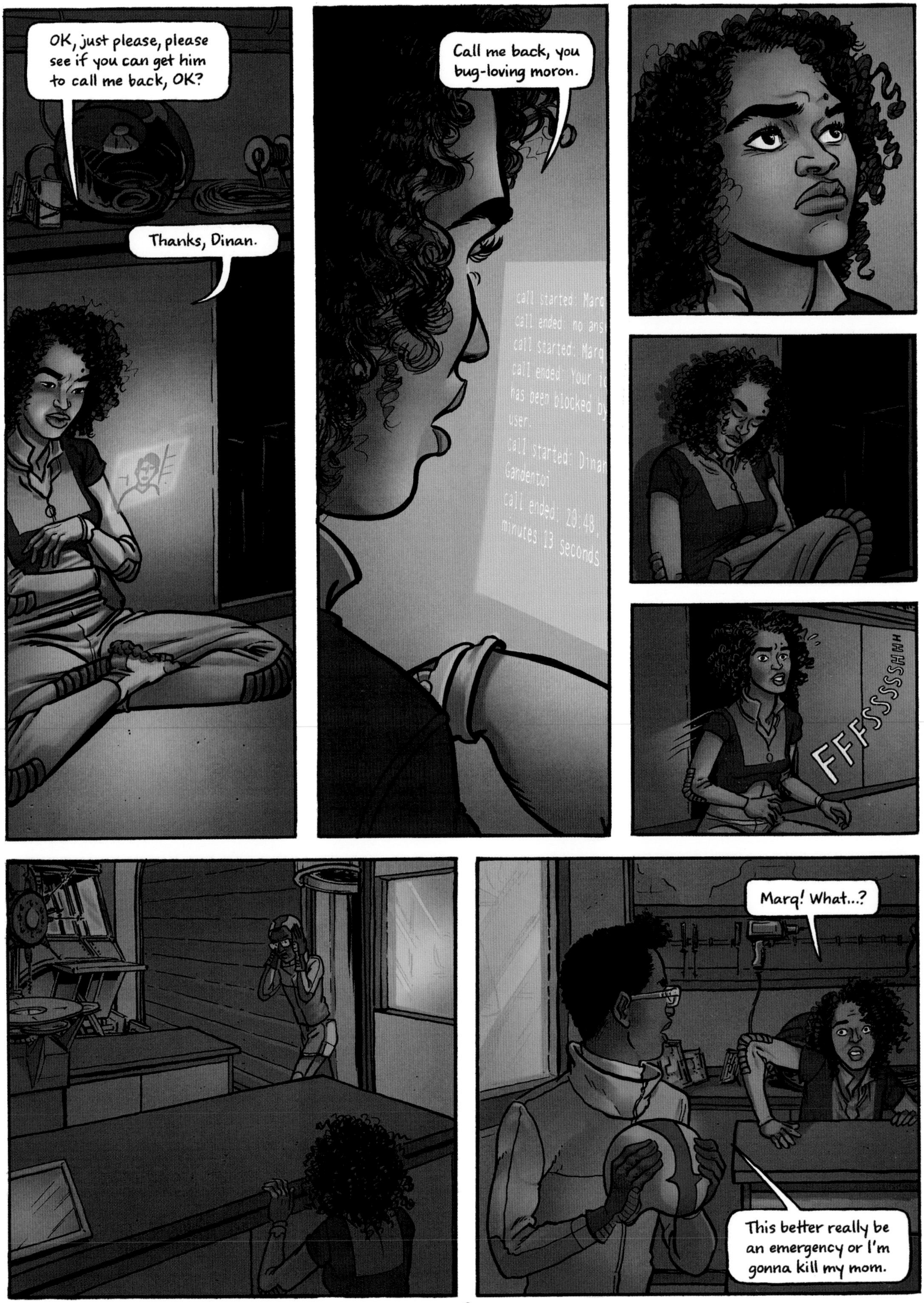
OK, just please, please see if you can get him to call me back, OK?
Thanks, Dinan.
Call me back, you bug-loving moron.
call started: Marq
call ended: no ans
call started: Marq
call ended: Your i
has been blocked by
user.
call started: Dinan
Gandentoi
call ended: 20:48,
minutes 13 seconds
FFFSSSSSHHH
Marq! What...?
This better really be an emergency or I'm gonna kill my mom.

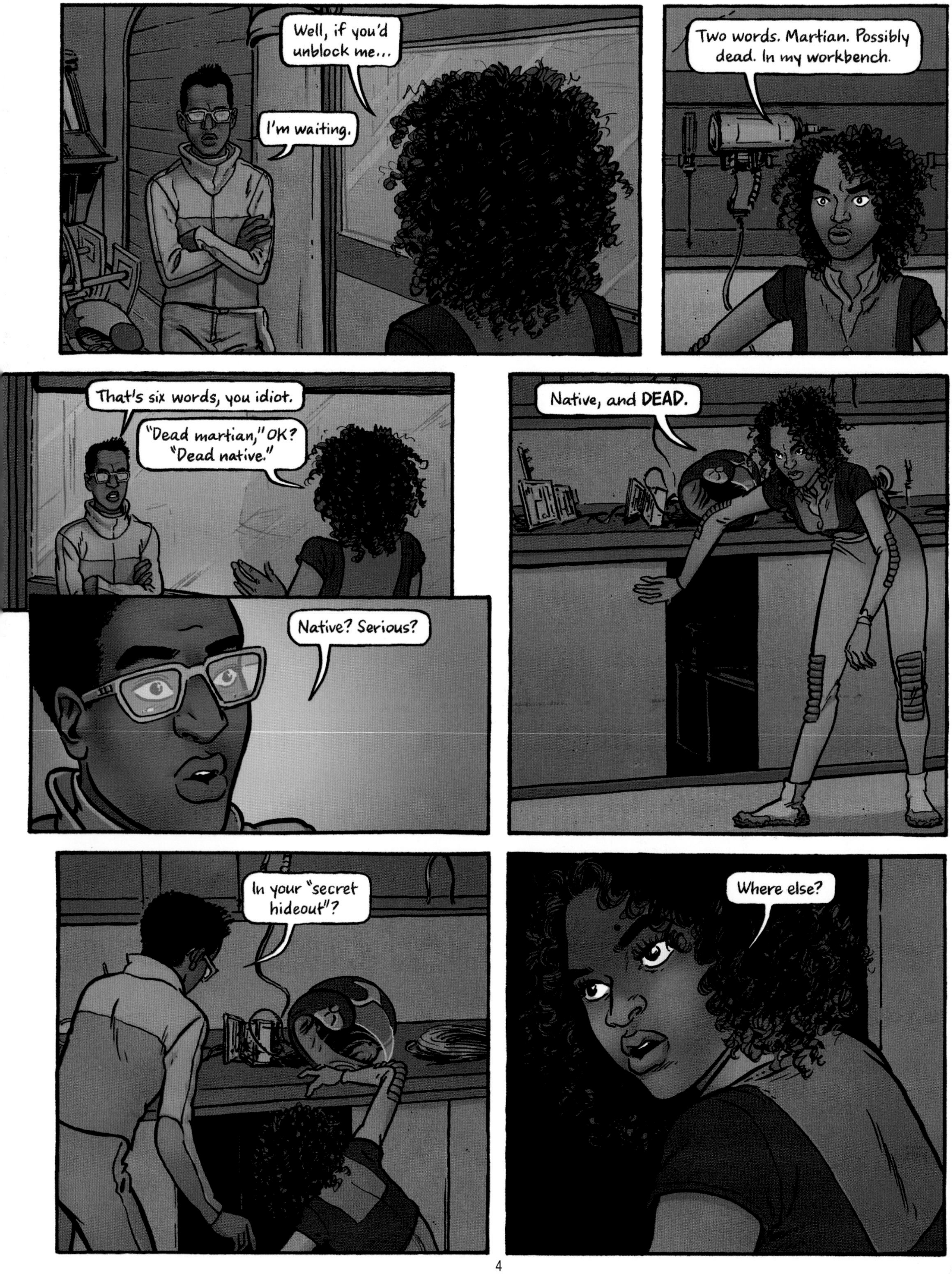
Well, if you'd unblock me...
I'm waiting.
Two words. Martian. Possibly dead. In my workbench.
That's six words, you idiot.
"Dead martian," OK? "Dead native."
Native? Serious?
Native, and DEAD.
In your "secret hideout"?
Where else?

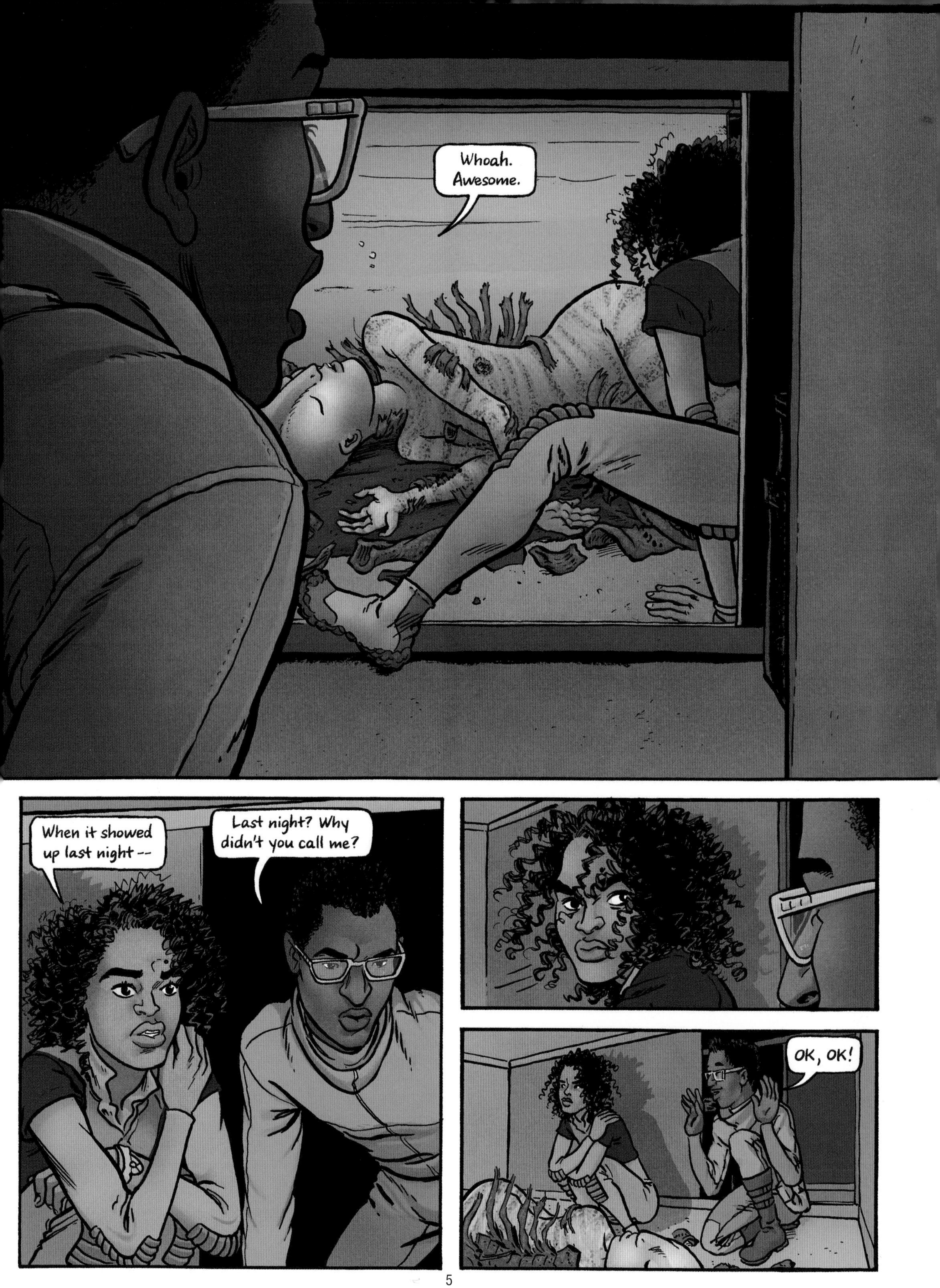
Whoah. Awesome.
When it showed up last night --
Last night? Why didn't you call me?
OK, OK!

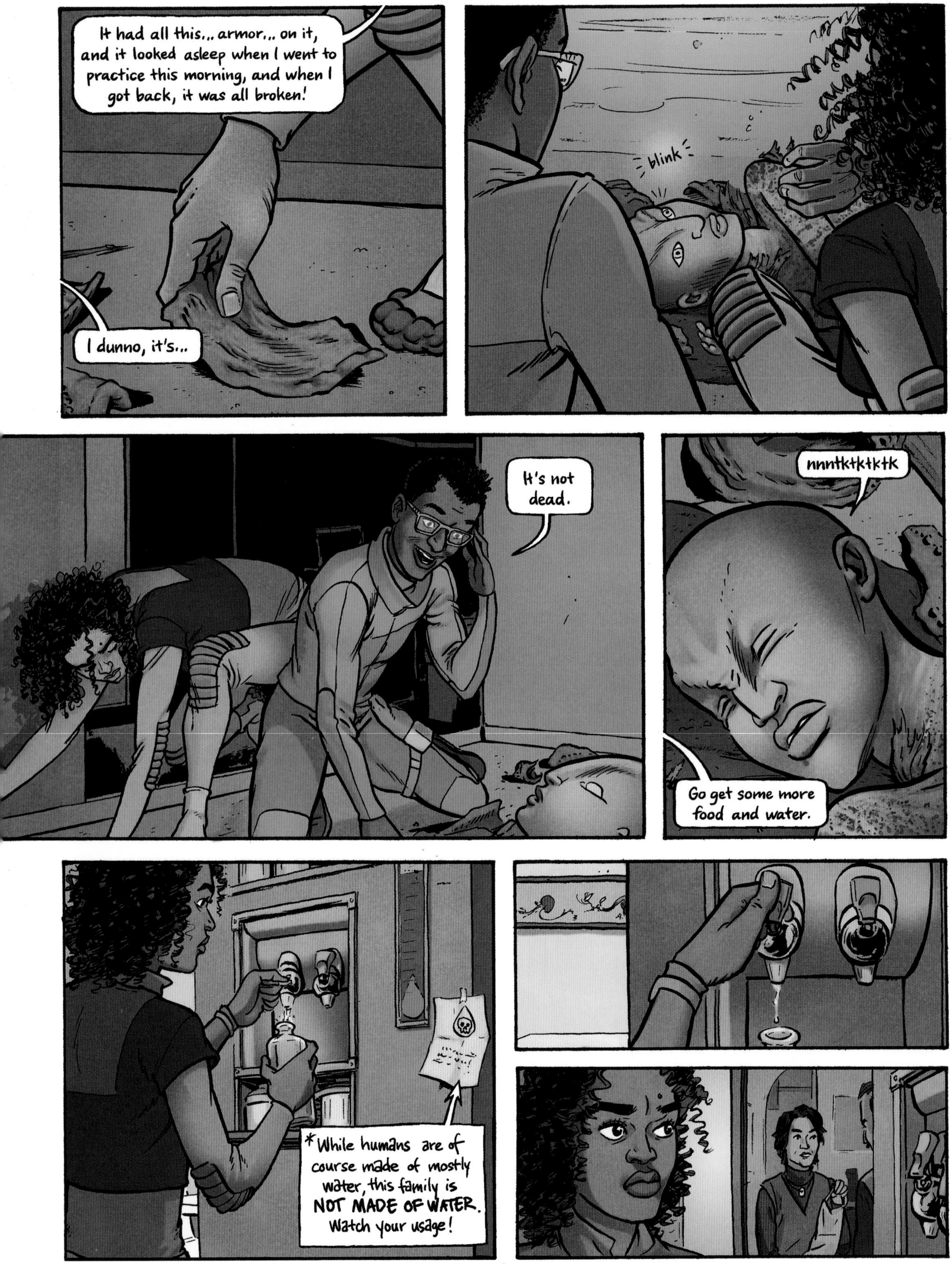
It had all this... armor... on it, and it looked asleep when I went to practice this morning, and when I got back, it was all broken!
I dunno, it's...
blink
It's not dead.
nnntktktktk
Go get some more food and water.
*While humans are of course made of mostly water, this family is NOT MADE OF WATER. Watch your usage!

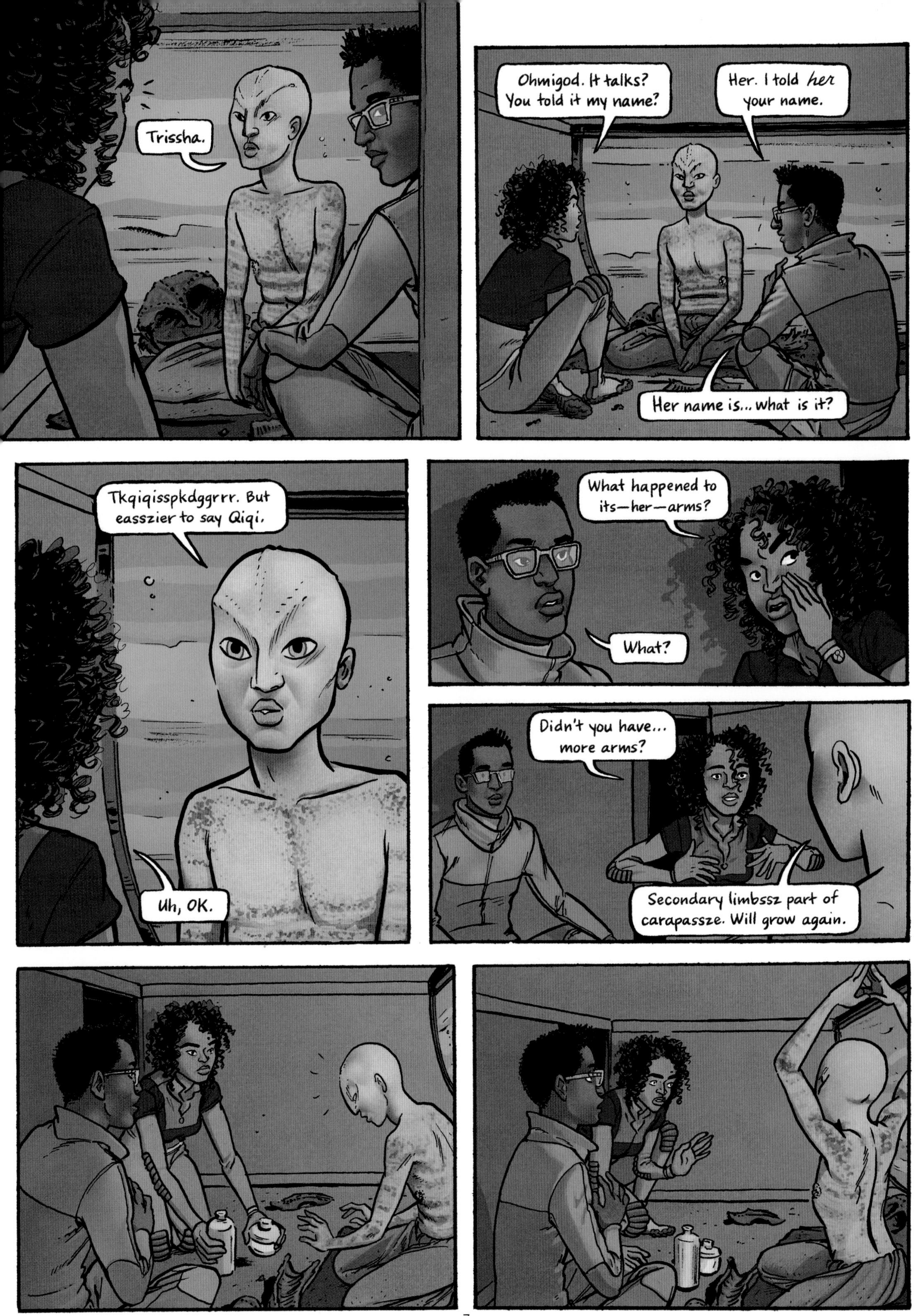

Trissha.
Ohmigod. It talks? You told it my name?
Her. I told her your name.
Her name is... what is it?
Tkqiqisspkdggrrr. But easszier to say Qiqi.
Uh, OK.
What happened to its—her—arms?
What?
Didn't you have... more arms?
Secondary limbssz part of carapassze. Will grow again.

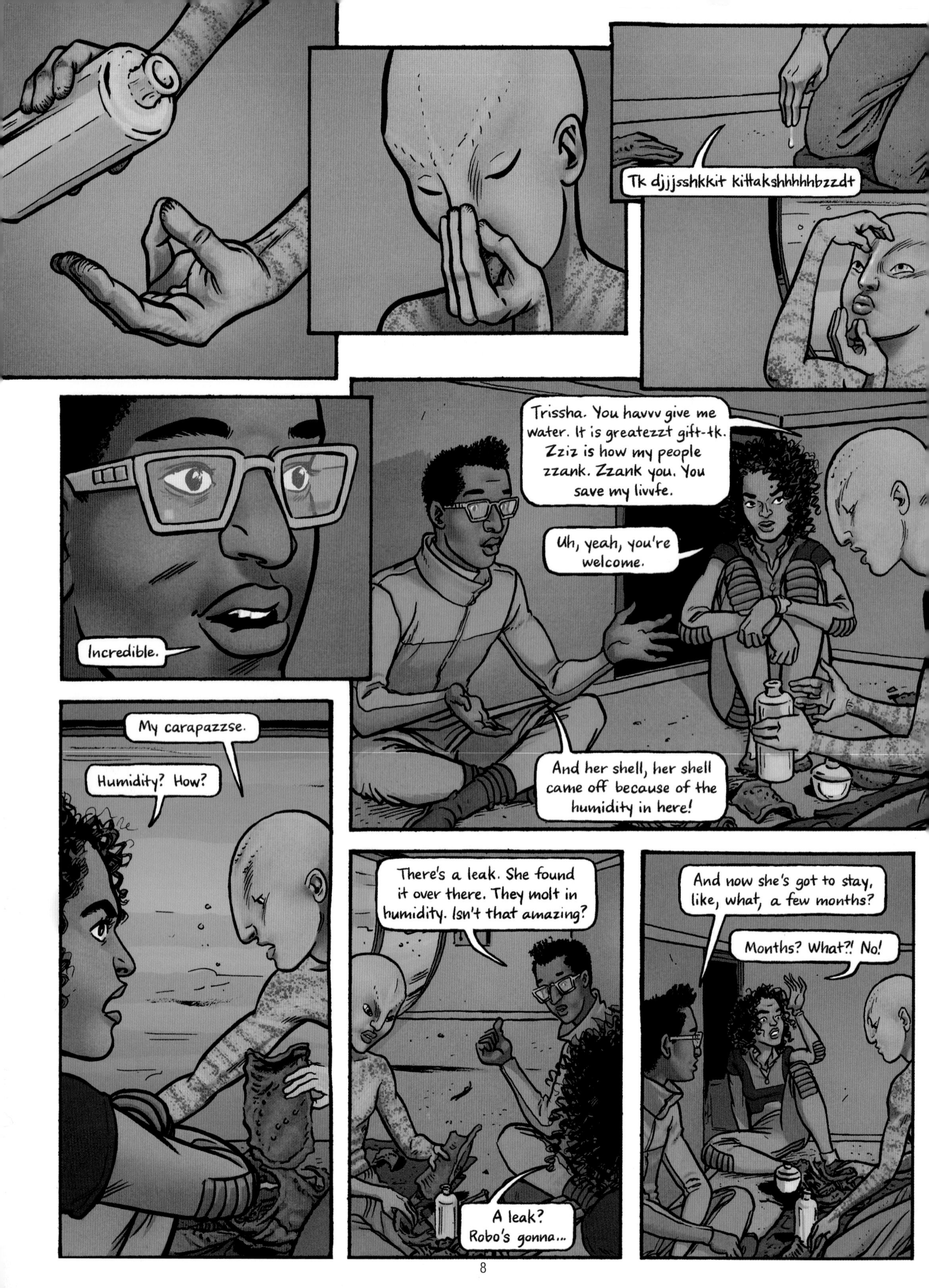
Tk djjjsshkkit kittakshhhhhbzzdt
Incredible.
Trissha. You havvv give me water. It is greatezzt gift-tk. Zziz is how my people zzank. Zzank you. You save my livvfe.
Uh, yeah, you're welcome.
And her shell, her shell came off because of the humidity in here!
My carapazzse.
Humidity? How?
There's a leak. She found it over there. They molt in humidity. Isn't that amazing?
A leak? Robo's gonna...
And now she's got to stay, like, what, a few months?
Months? What?! No!

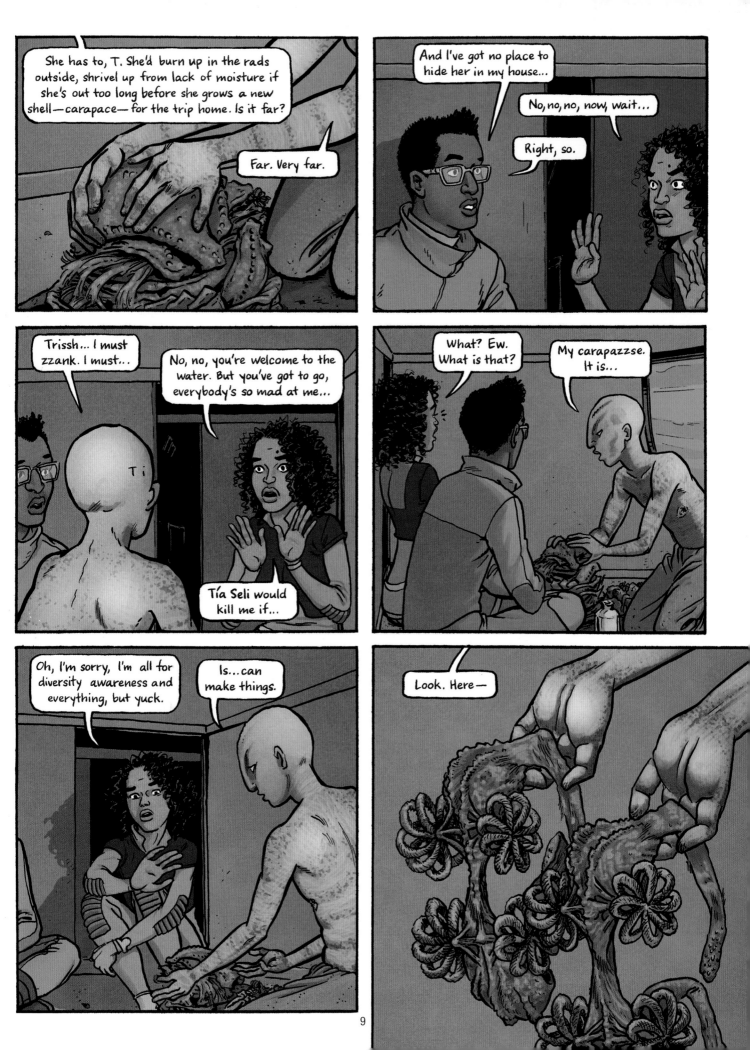

She has to, T. She'd burn up in the rads outside, shrivel up from lack of moisture if she's out too long before she grows a new shell—carapace— for the trip home. Is it far?

Far. Very far.

And I've got no place to hide her in my house...

No, no, no, now, wait...

Right, so.

Trissh... I must zzank. I must...

No, no, you're welcome to the water. But you've got to go, everybody's so mad at me...

Tía Seli would kill me if...

What? Ew. What is that?

My carapazzse. It is...

Oh, I'm sorry, I'm all for diversity awareness and everything, but yuck.

Is...can make things.

Look. Here—

9

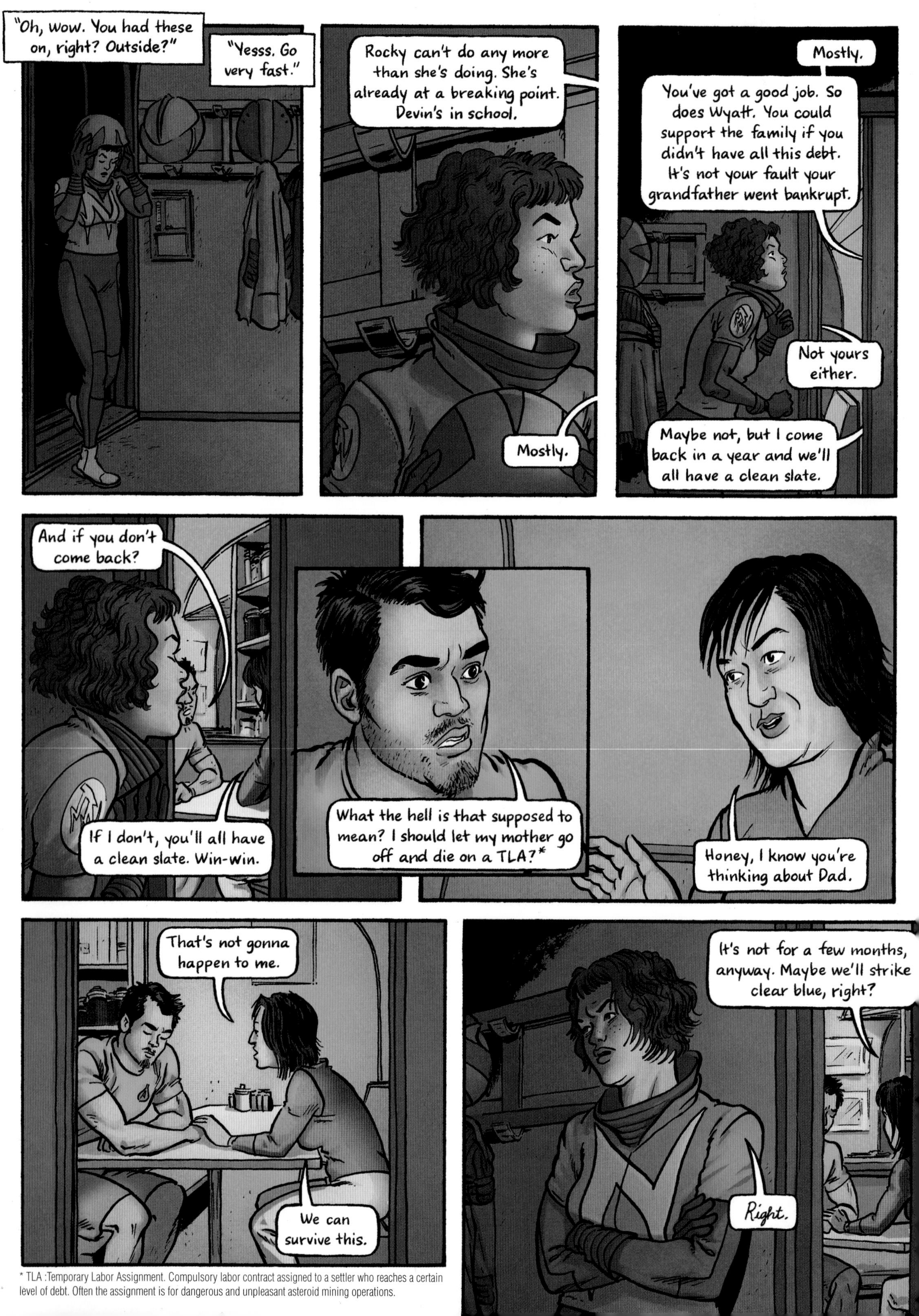
"Oh, wow. You had these on, right? Outside?"
"Yesss. Go very fast."
Rocky can't do any more than she's doing. She's already at a breaking point. Devin's in school.
Mostly.
Mostly.
You've got a good job. So does Wyatt. You could support the family if you didn't have all this debt. It's not your fault your grandfather went bankrupt.
Not yours either.
Maybe not, but I come back in a year and we'll all have a clean slate.
And if you don't come back?
If I don't, you'll all have a clean slate. Win-win.
What the hell is that supposed to mean? I should let my mother go off and die on a TLA?*
Honey, I know you're thinking about Dad.
That's not gonna happen to me.
We can survive this.
It's not for a few months, anyway. Maybe we'll strike clear blue, right?
Right.

* TLA :Temporary Labor Assignment. Compulsory labor contract assigned to a settler who reaches a certain level of debt. Often the assignment is for dangerous and unpleasant asteroid mining operations.

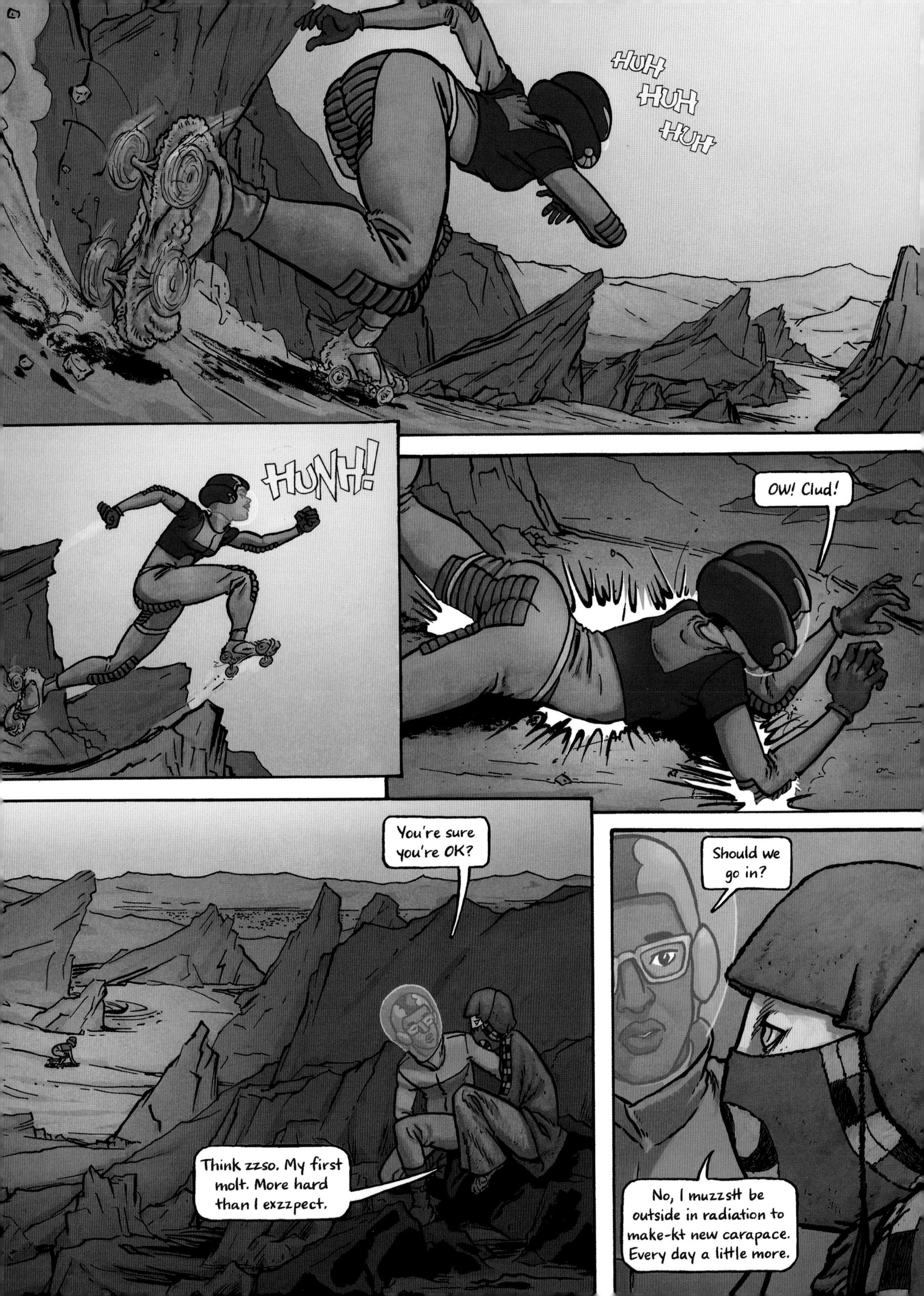
HUH HUH HUH
HUNH!
OW! Clud!
You're sure you're OK?
Think zzso. My first molt. More hard than I exzzpect.
Should we go in?
No, I muzzsH be outside in radiation to make-kt new carapace. Every day a little more.

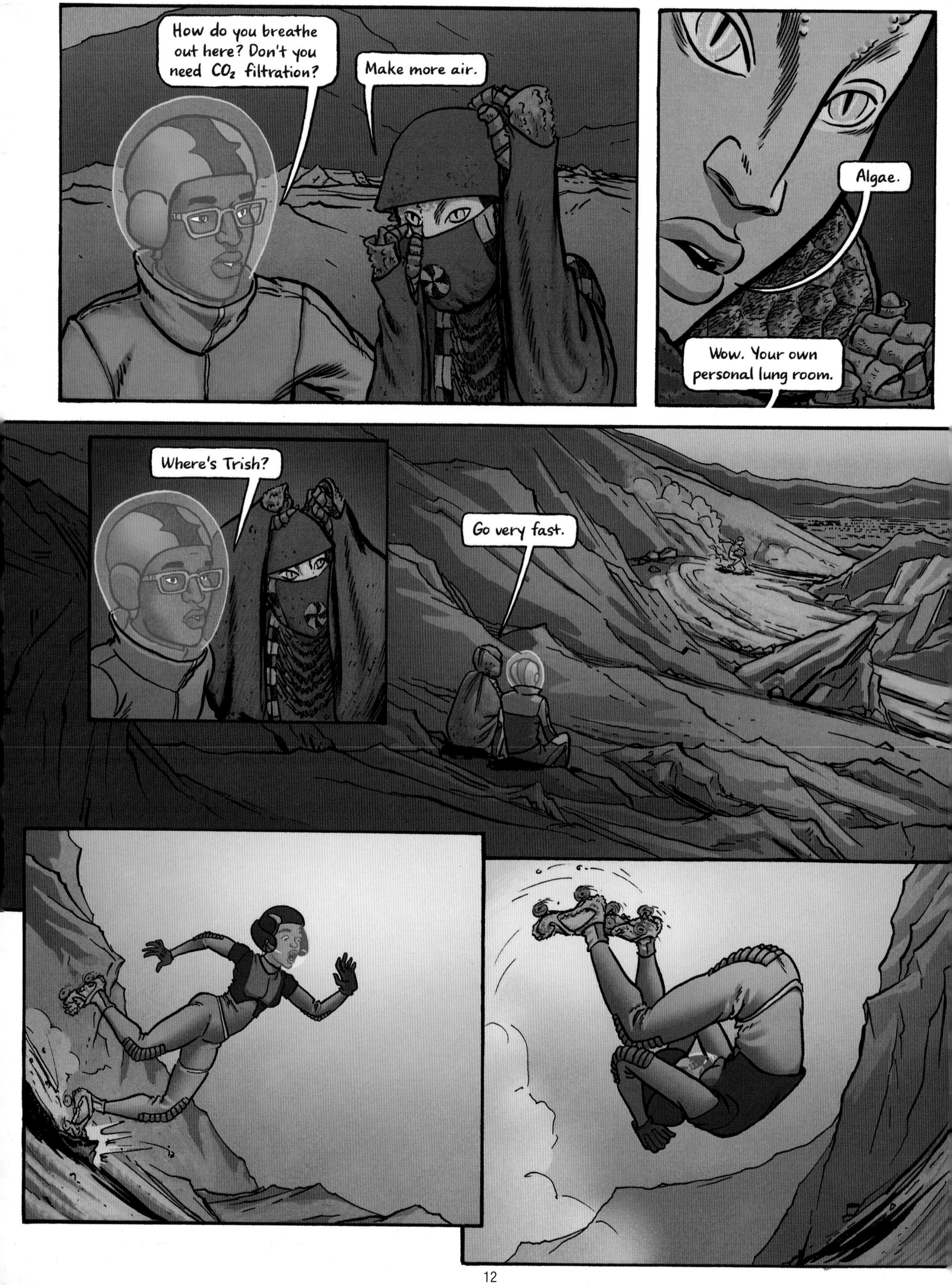
How do you breathe out here? Don't you need CO_2 filtration?
Make more air.
Algae.
Wow. Your own personal lung room.
Where's Trish?
Go very fast.

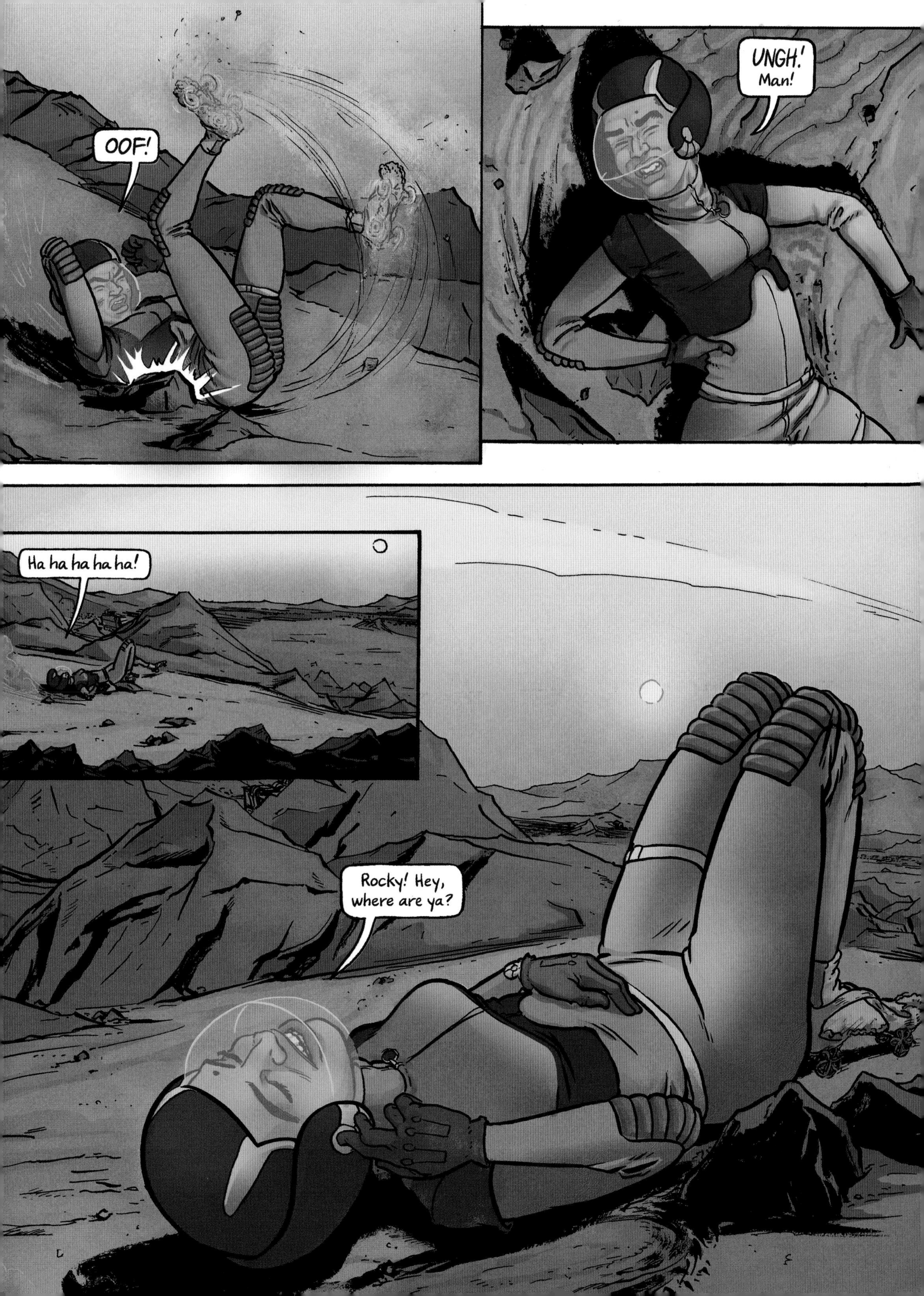

OOF!
UNGH! Man!
Ha ha ha ha ha!
Rocky! Hey, where are ya?

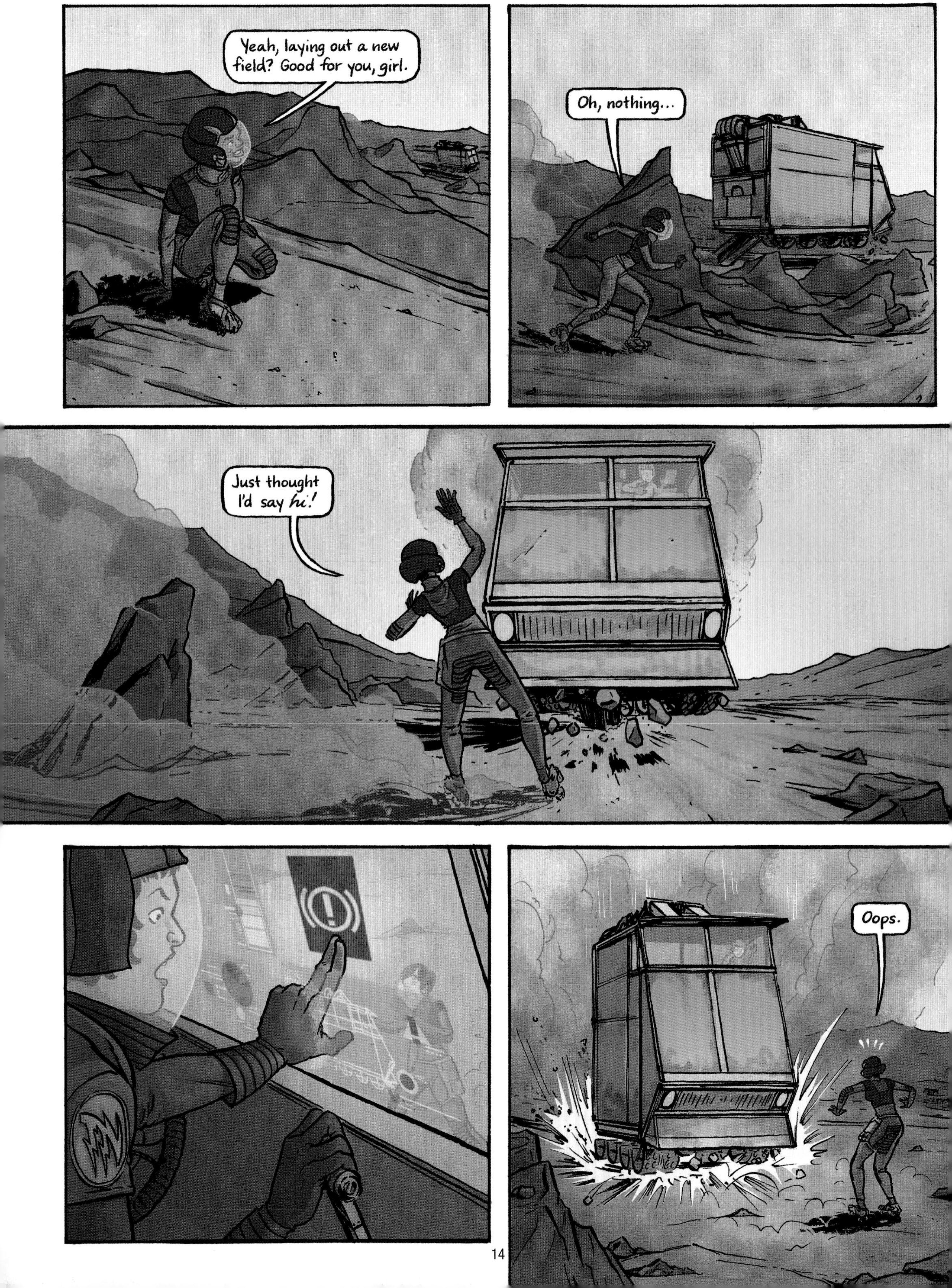

Yeah, laying out a new field? Good for you, girl.
Oh, nothing...
Just thought I'd say hi!
Oops.

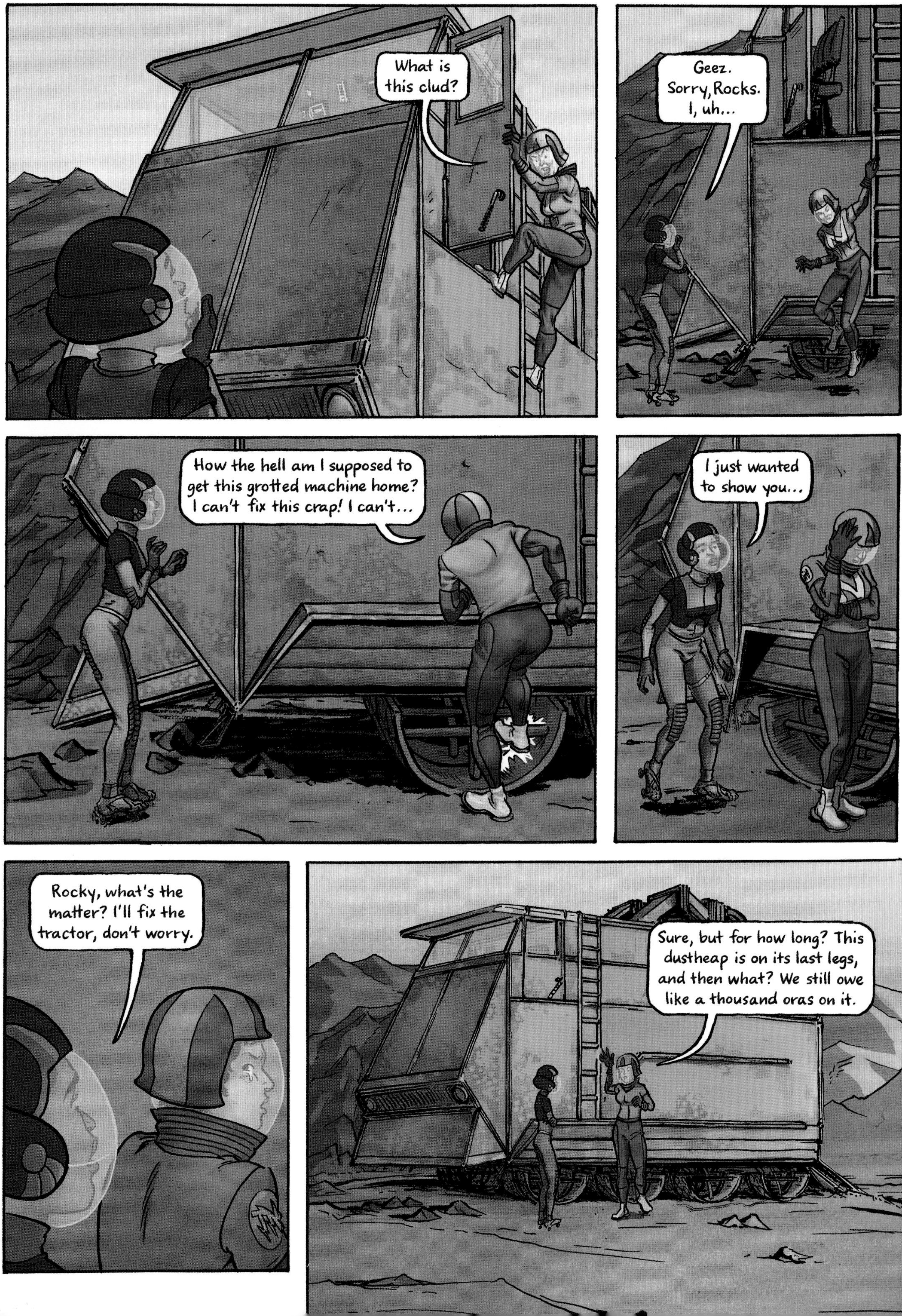
What is this clud?
Geez. Sorry, Rocks. I, uh...
How the hell am I supposed to get this grotted machine home? I can't fix this crap! I can't...
I just wanted to show you...
Rocky, what's the matter? I'll fix the tractor, don't worry.
Sure, but for how long? This dustheap is on its last legs, and then what? We still owe like a thousand oras on it.

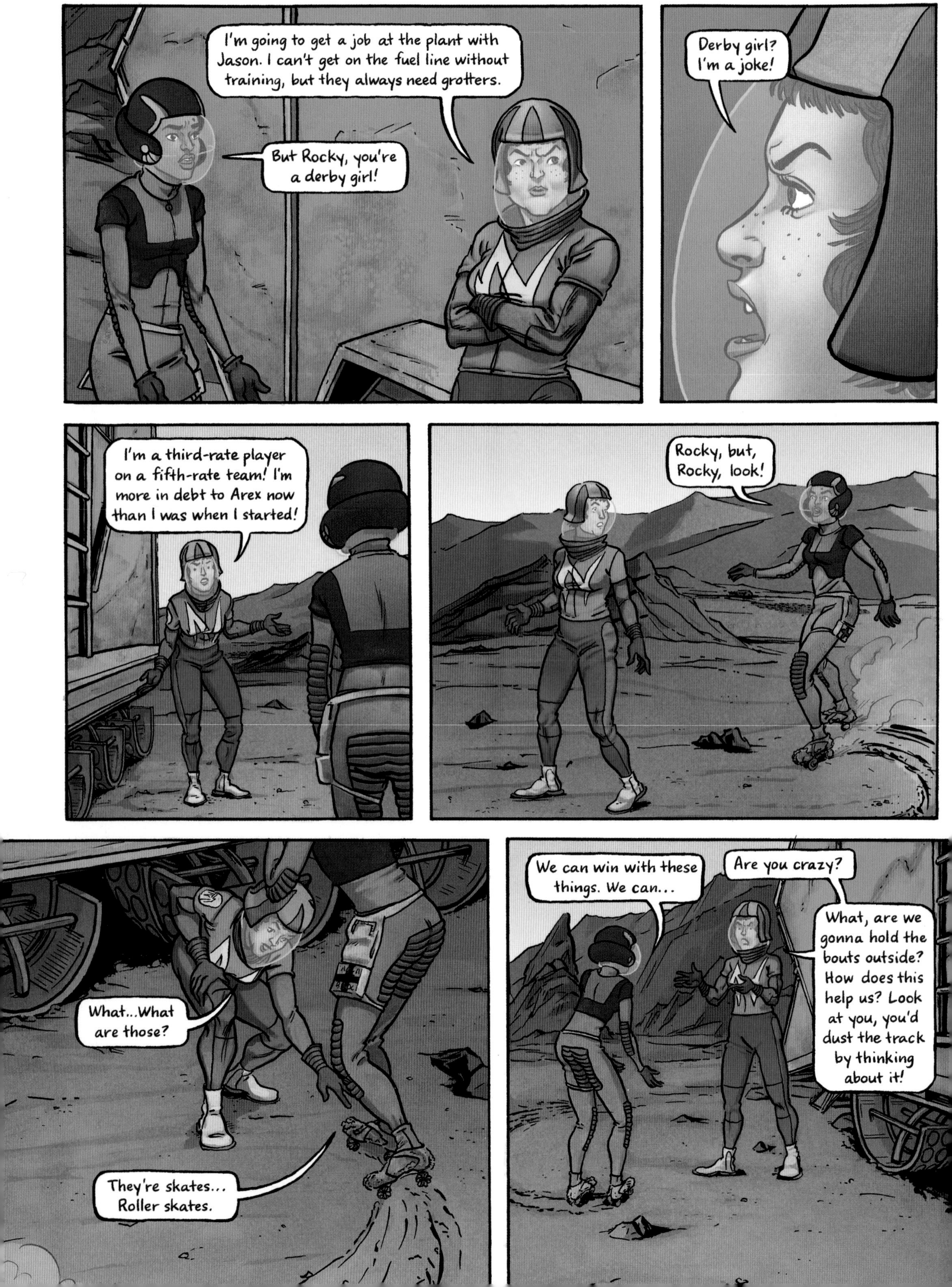
I'm going to get a job at the plant with Jason. I can't get on the fuel line without training, but they always need grotters.
But Rocky, you're a derby girl!
Derby girl? I'm a joke!
I'm a third-rate player on a fifth-rate team! I'm more in debt to Arex now than I was when I started!
Rocky, but, Rocky, look!
What...What are those?
They're skates... Roller skates.
We can win with these things. We can...
Are you crazy?
What, are we gonna hold the bouts outside? How does this help us? Look at you, you'd dust the track by thinking about it!

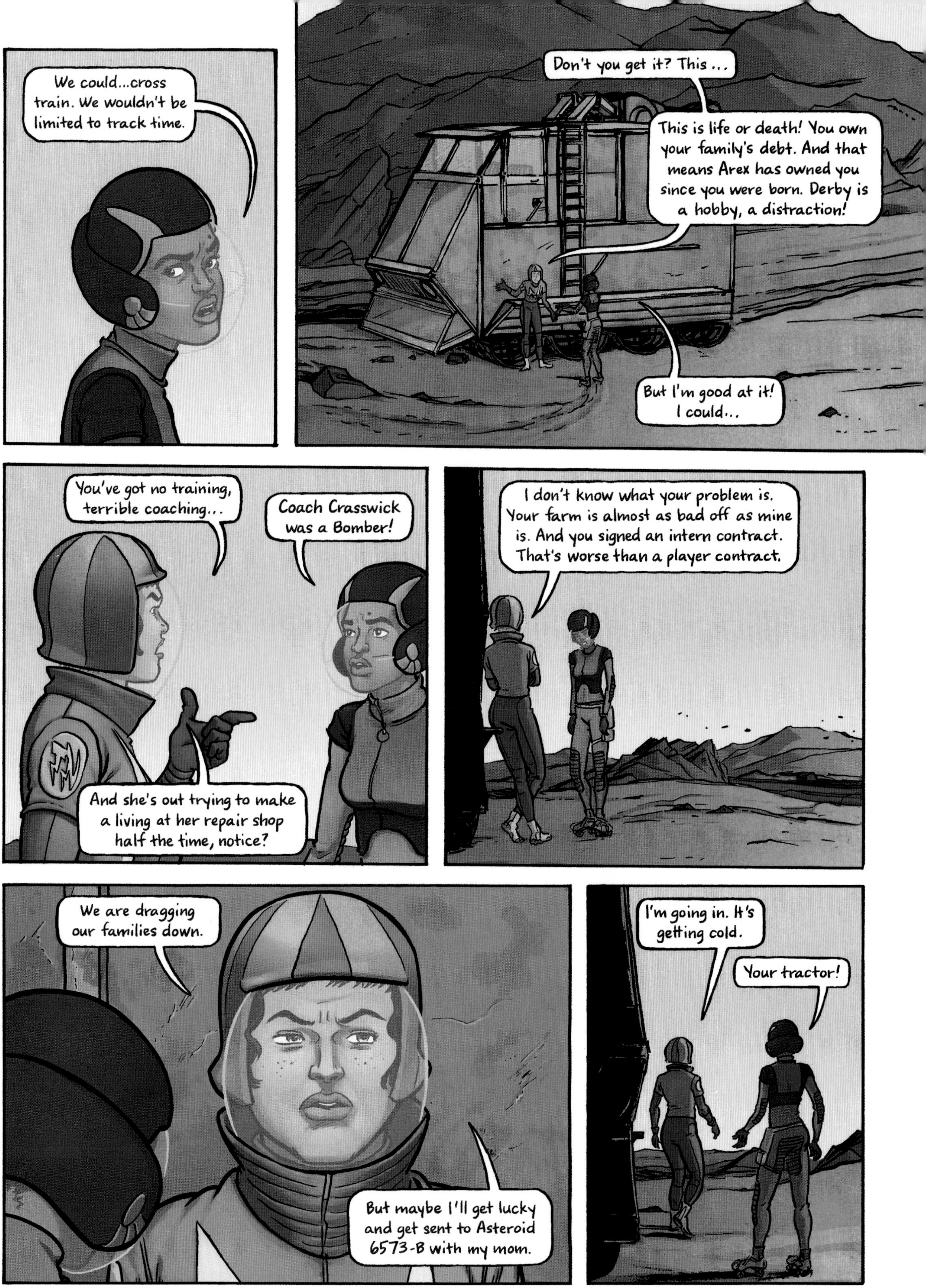

We could...cross train. We wouldn't be limited to track time.
Don't you get it? This...
This is life or death! You own your family's debt. And that means Arex has owned you since you were born. Derby is a hobby, a distraction!
But I'm good at it! I could...
You've got no training, terrible coaching...
Coach Crasswick was a Bomber!
And she's out trying to make a living at her repair shop half the time, notice?
I don't know what your problem is. Your farm is almost as bad off as mine is. And you signed an intern contract. That's worse than a player contract.
We are dragging our families down.
But maybe I'll get lucky and get sent to Asteroid 6573-B with my mom.
I'm going in. It's getting cold.
Your tractor!

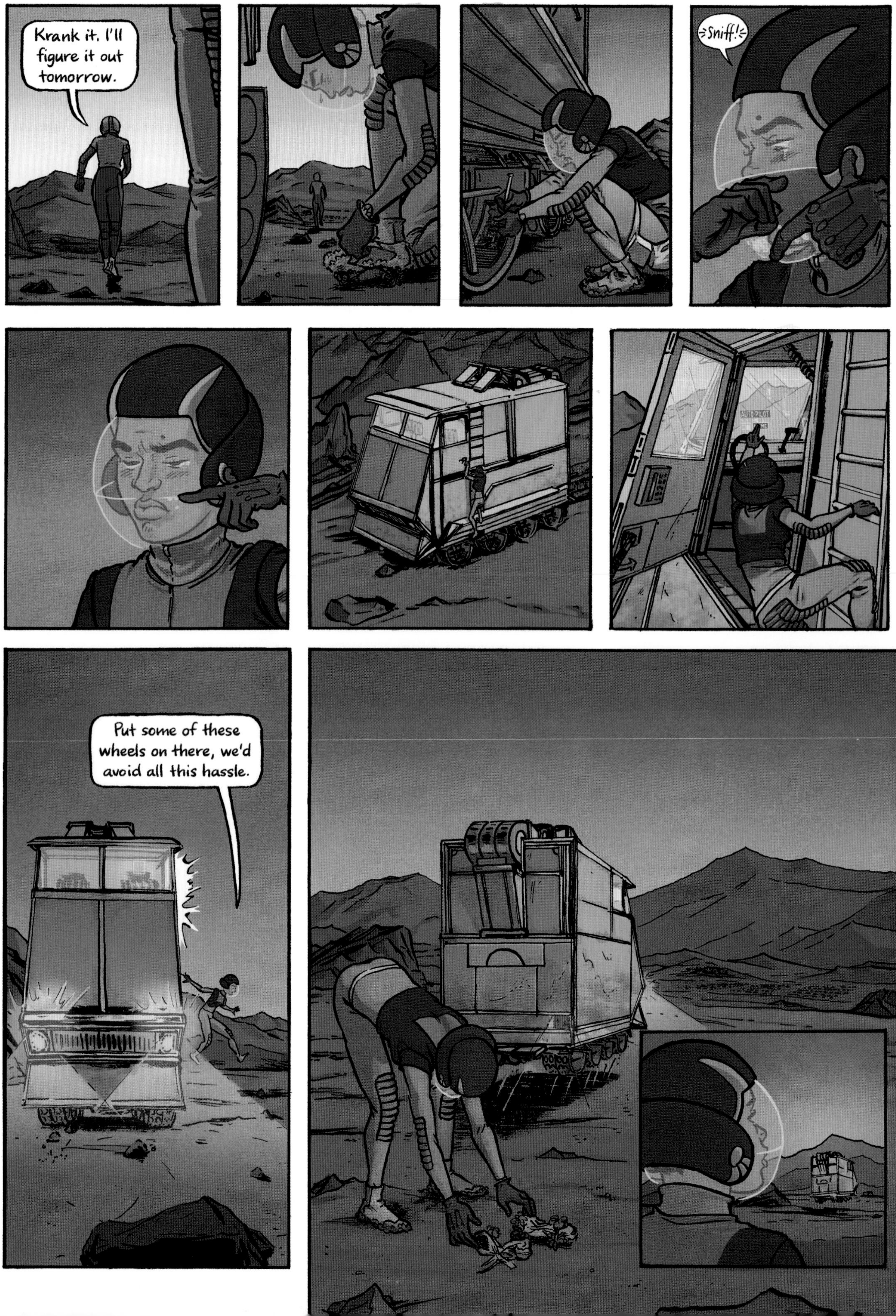
Krank it. I'll figure it out tomorrow.
Sniff!
Put some of these wheels on there, we'd avoid all this hassle.

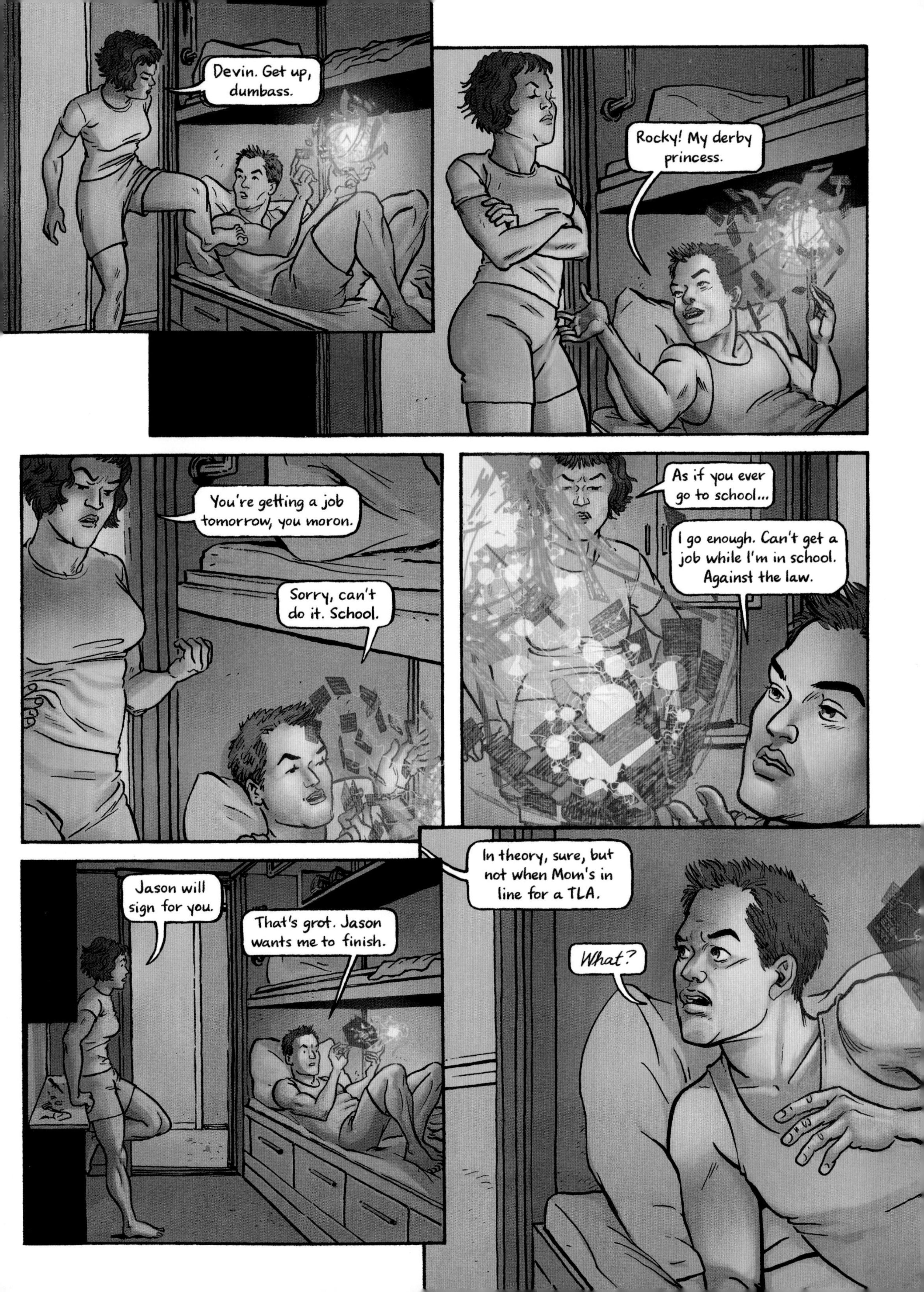
Devin. Get up, dumbass.
Rocky! My derby princess.
You're getting a job tomorrow, you moron.
Sorry, can't do it. School.
As if you ever go to school...
I go enough. Can't get a job while I'm in school. Against the law.
Jason will sign for you.
That's grot. Jason wants me to finish.
In theory, sure, but not when Mom's in line for a TLA.
What?

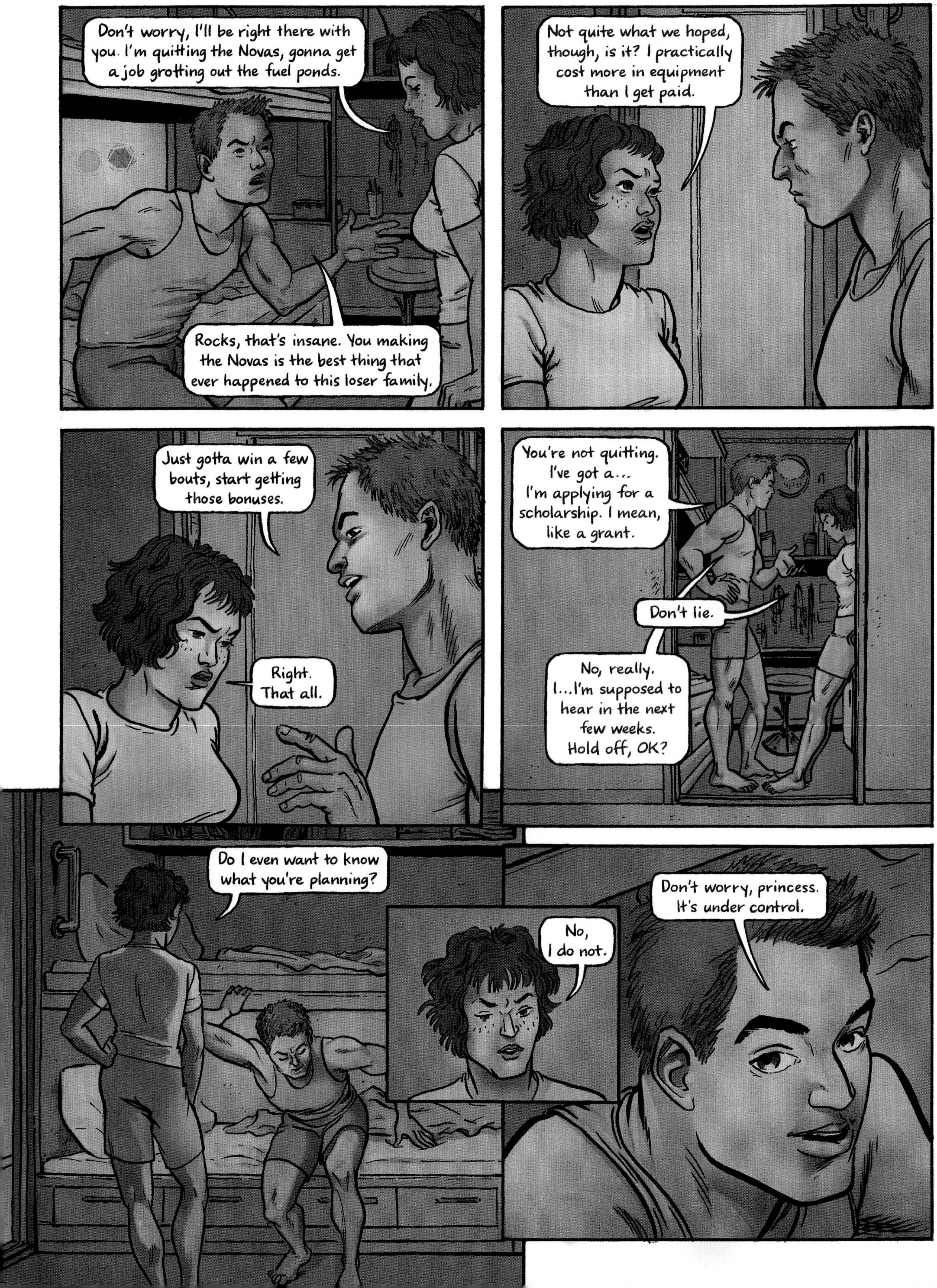
Don't worry, I'll be right there with you. I'm quitting the Novas, gonna get a job grotting out the fuel ponds.
Rocks, that's insane. You making the Novas is the best thing that ever happened to this loser family.
Not quite what we hoped, though, is it? I practically cost more in equipment than I get paid.
Just gotta win a few bouts, start getting those bonuses.
Right. That all.
You're not quitting. I've got a... I'm applying for a scholarship. I mean, like a grant.
Don't lie.
No, really. I...I'm supposed to hear in the next few weeks. Hold off, OK?
Do I even want to know what you're planning?
No, I do not.
Don't worry, princess. It's under control.

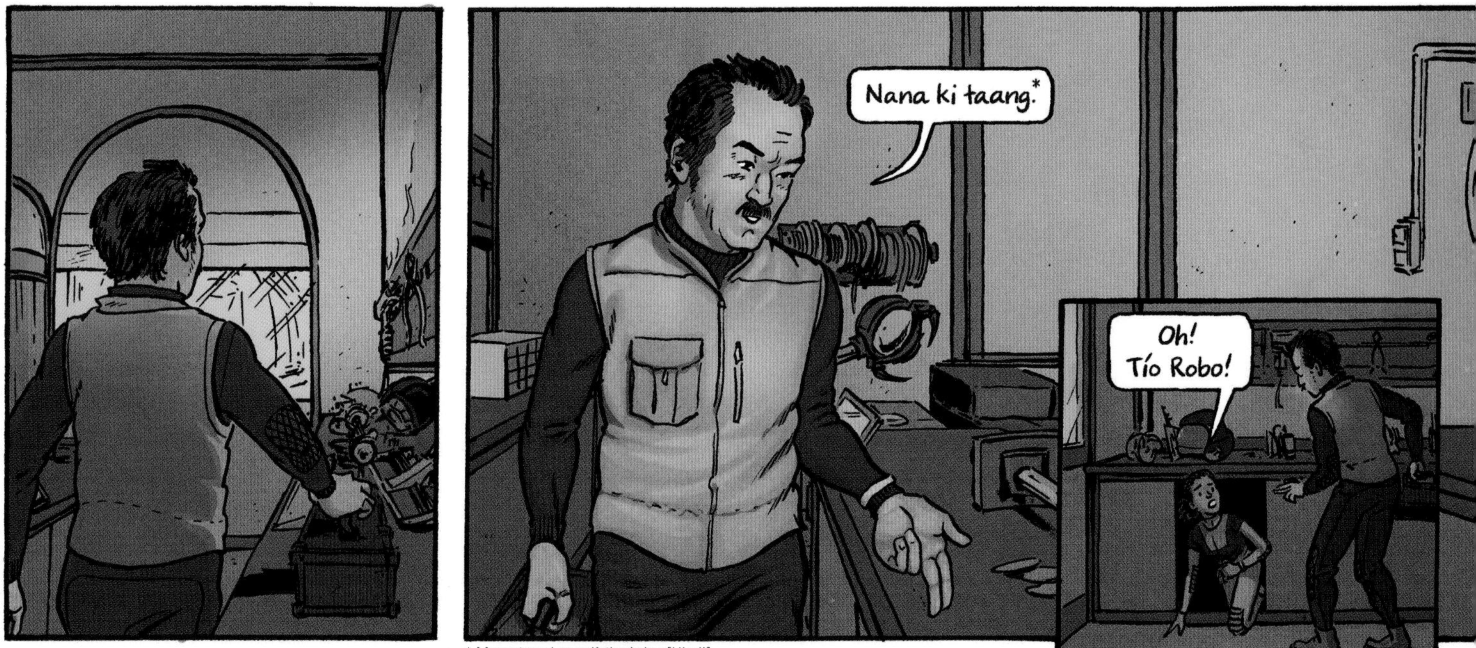
Nana ki taang.*
Oh! Tío Robo!

* My maternal grandfather's leg [Hindi]

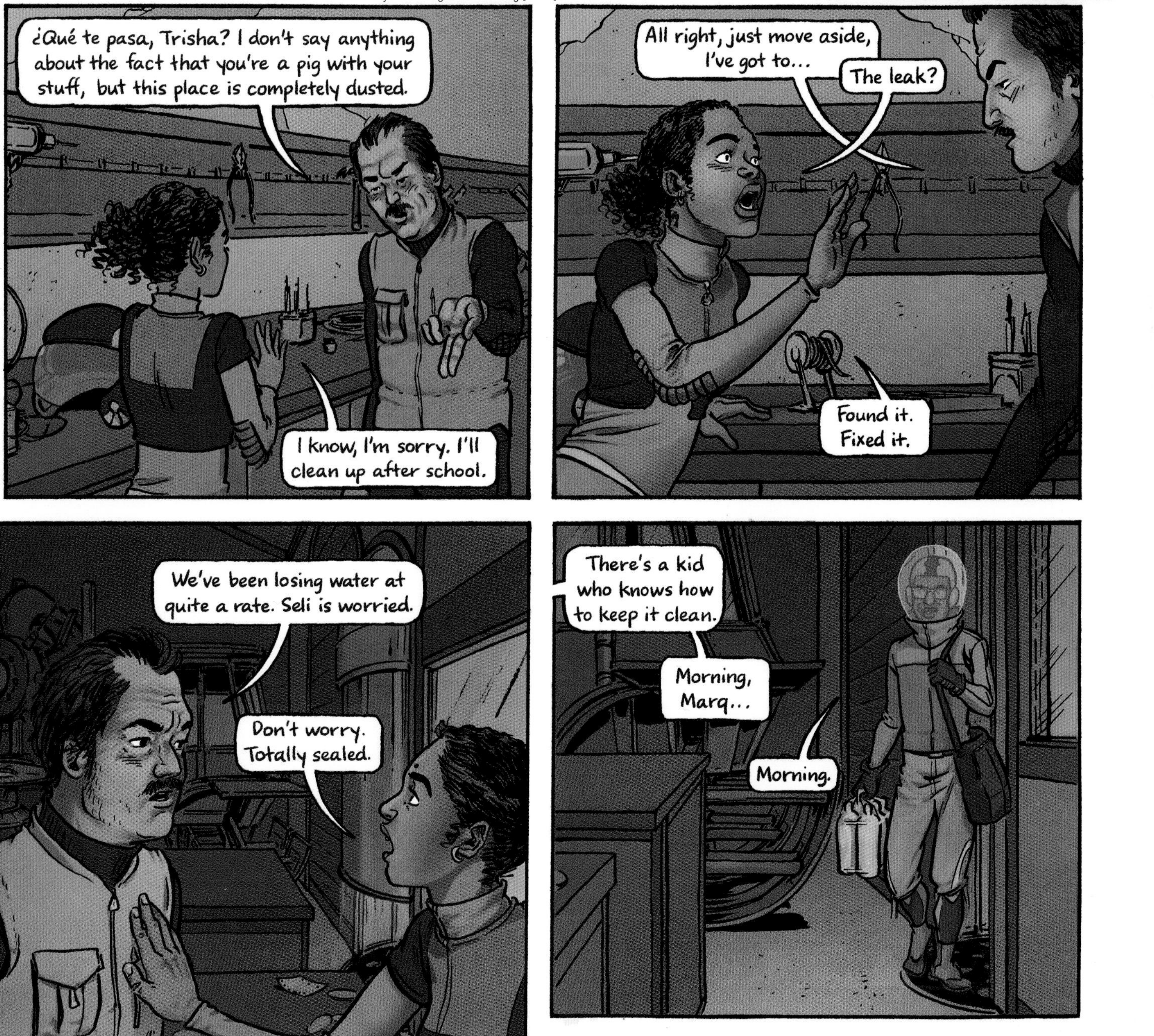
¿Qué te pasa, Trisha? I don't say anything about the fact that you're a pig with your stuff, but this place is completely dusted.
I know, I'm sorry. I'll clean up after school.
All right, just move aside, I've got to...
The leak?
Found it. Fixed it.
We've been losing water at quite a rate. Seli is worried.
Don't worry. Totally sealed.
There's a kid who knows how to keep it clean.
Morning, Marq...
Morning.

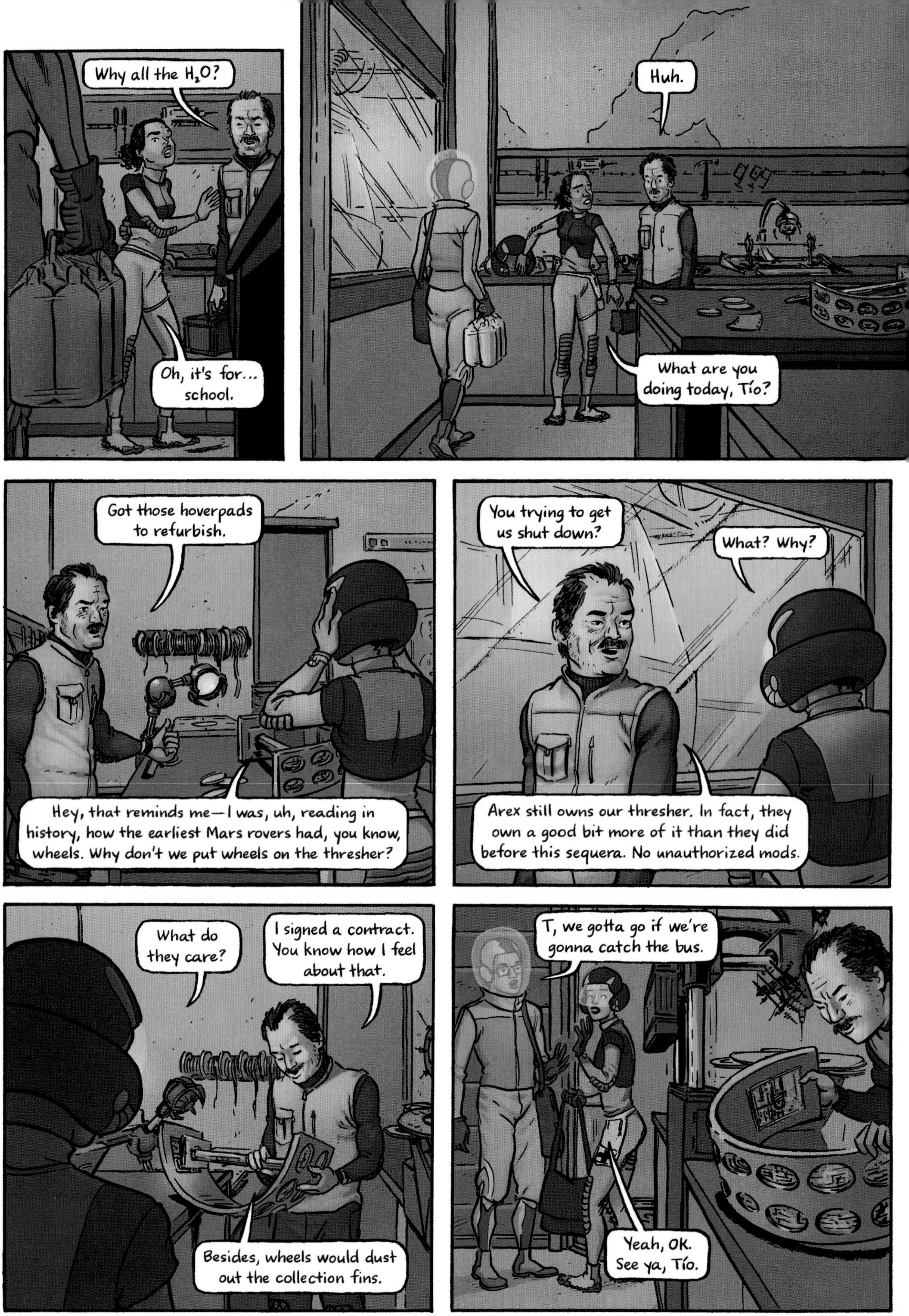
Why all the H_2O?
Oh, it's for... school.
Huh.
What are you doing today, Tío?
Got those hoverpads to refurbish.
Hey, that reminds me—I was, uh, reading in history, how the earliest Mars rovers had, you know, wheels. Why don't we put wheels on the thresher?
You trying to get us shut down?
What? Why?
Arex still owns our thresher. In fact, they own a good bit more of it than they did before this sequera. No unauthorized mods.
What do they care?
I signed a contract. You know how I feel about that.
Besides, wheels would dust out the collection fins.
T, we gotta go if we're gonna catch the bus.
Yeah, OK. See ya, Tío.

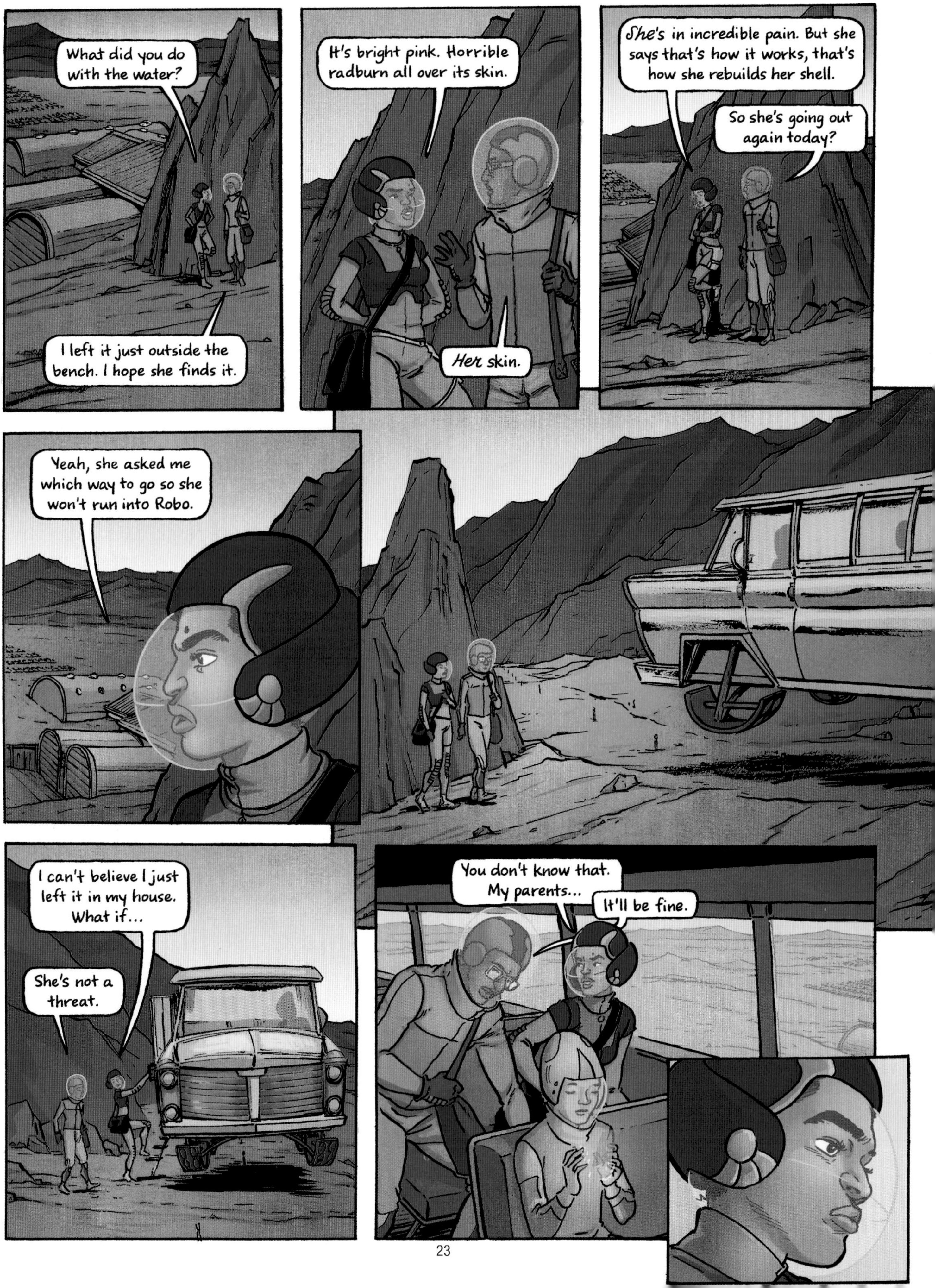
What did you do with the water?
I left it just outside the bench. I hope she finds it.
It's bright pink. Horrible radburn all over its skin.
Her skin.
She's in incredible pain. But she says that's how it works, that's how she rebuilds her shell.
So she's going out again today?
Yeah, she asked me which way to go so she won't run into Robo.
I can't believe I just left it in my house. What if...
She's not a threat.
You don't know that. My parents...
It'll be fine.

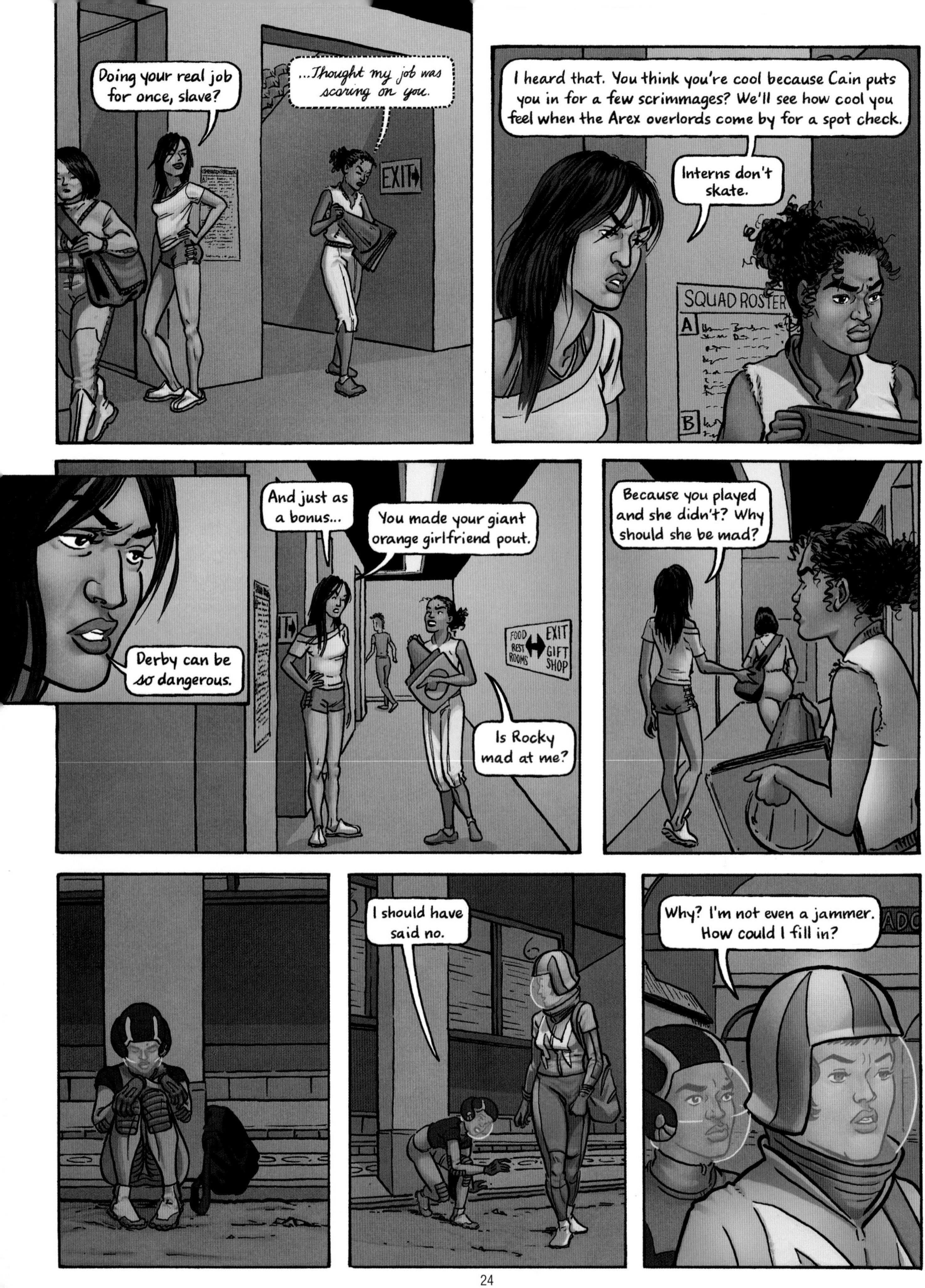
Doing your real job for once, slave?
...Thought my job was scoring on you.
I heard that. You think you're cool because Cain puts you in for a few scrimmages? We'll see how cool you feel when the Arex overlords come by for a spot check.
Interns don't skate.
SQUAD ROSTER
EXIT
Derby can be so dangerous.
And just as a bonus...
You made your giant orange girlfriend pout.
Is Rocky mad at me?
FOOD REST ROOMS
EXIT GIFT SHOP
Because you played and she didn't? Why should she be mad?
I should have said no.
Why? I'm not even a jammer. How could I fill in?

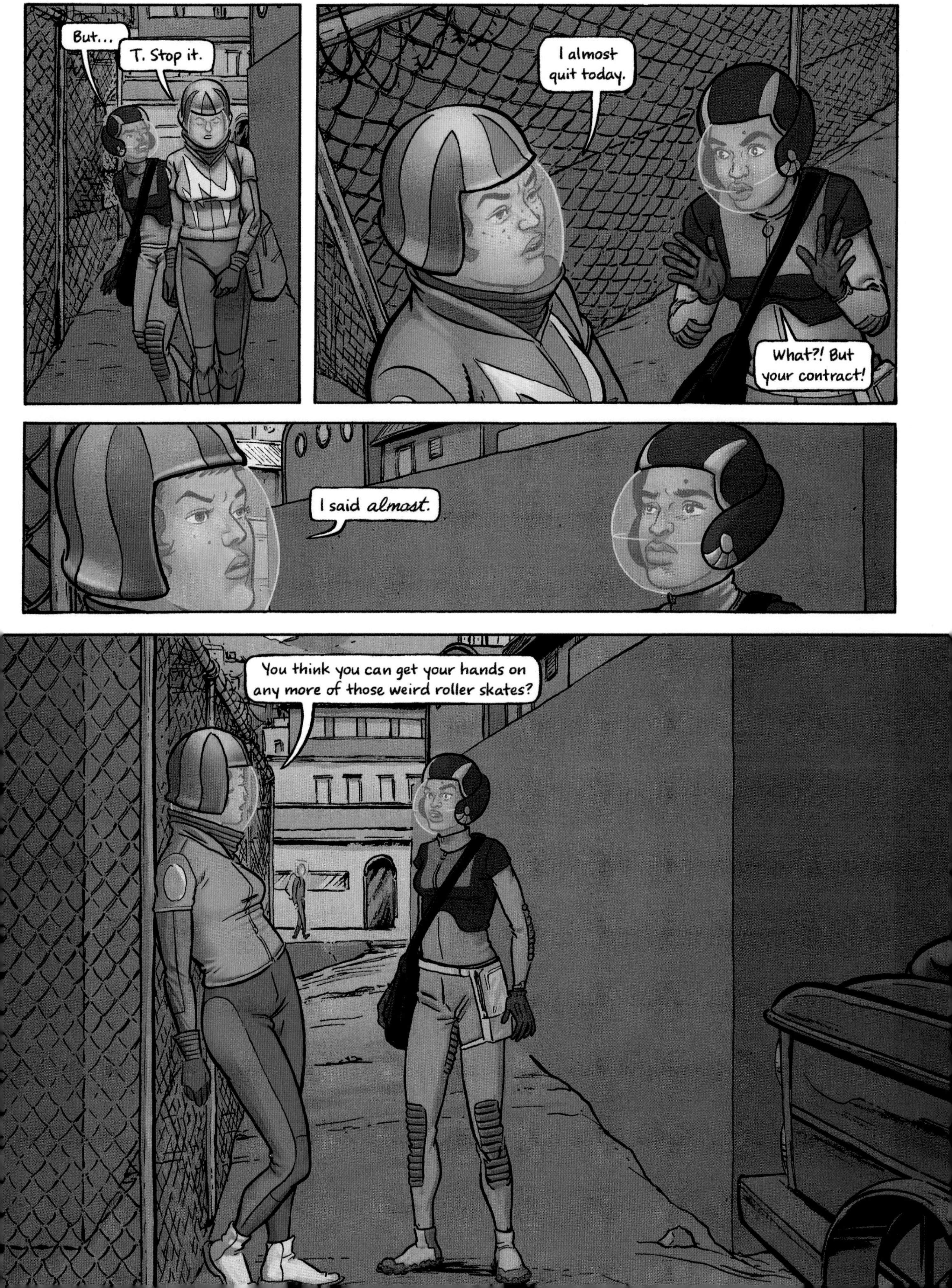
But...
T. Stop it.
I almost quit today.
What?! But your contract!
I said *almost*.
You think you can get your hands on any more of those weird roller skates?

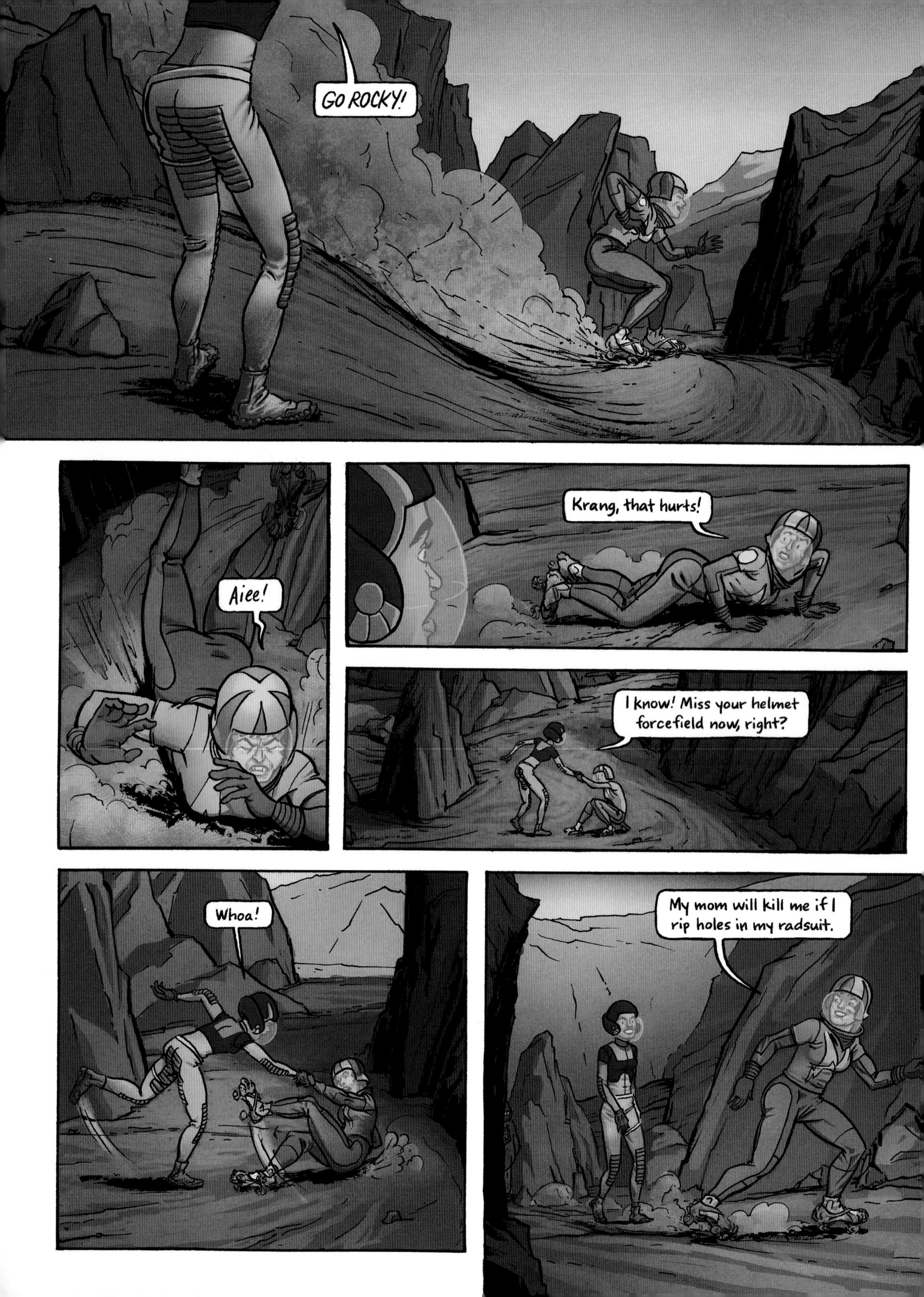
GO ROCKY!
Aiee!
Krang, that hurts!
I know! Miss your helmet forcefield now, right?
Whoa!
My mom will kill me if I rip holes in my radsuit.

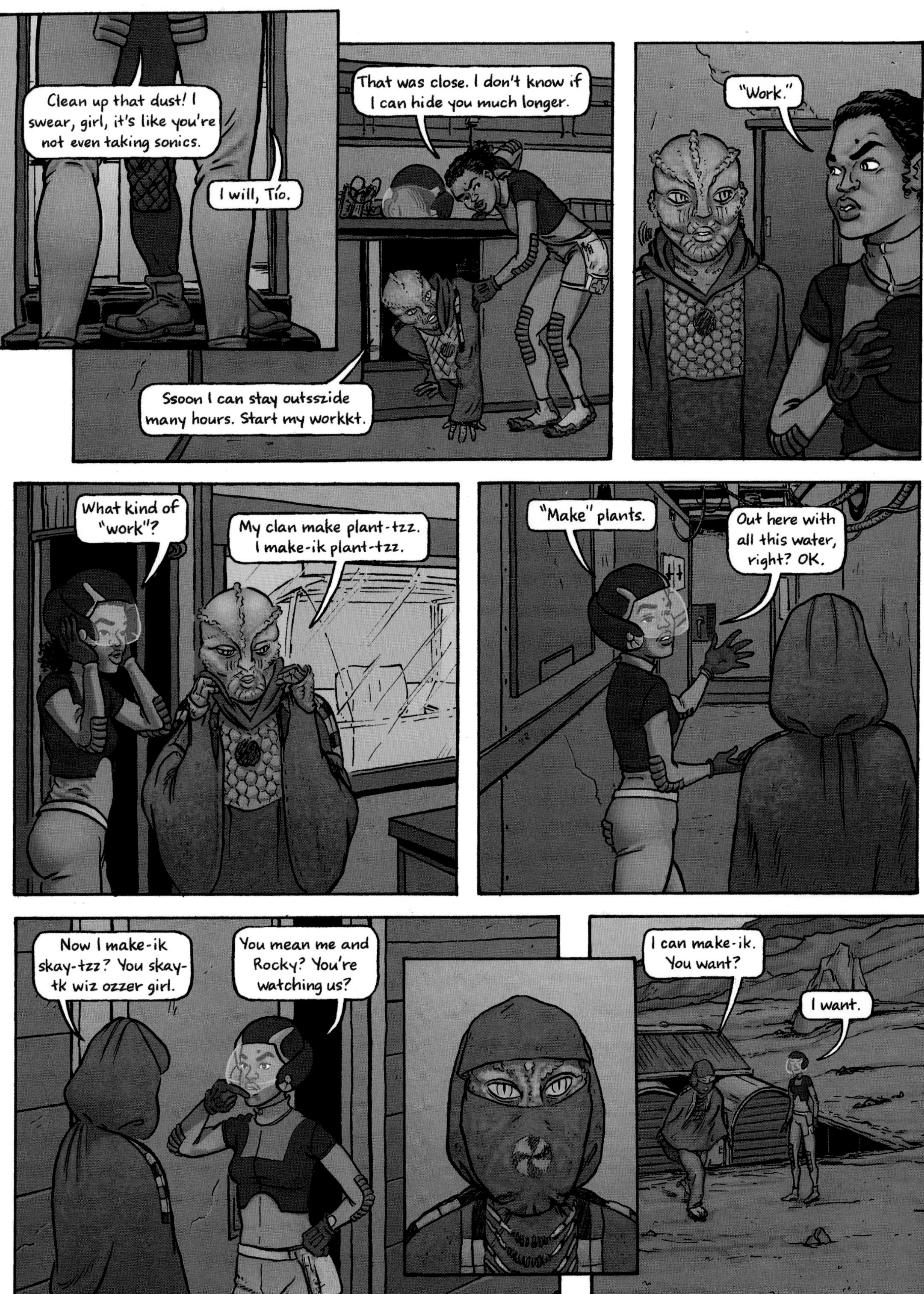
Clean up that dust! I swear, girl, it's like you're not even taking sonics.
I will, Tío.
That was close. I don't know if I can hide you much longer.
Ssoon I can stay outsszide many hours. Start my workkt.
"Work."
What kind of "work"?
My clan make plant-tzz. I make-ik plant-tzz.
"Make" plants.
Out here with all this water, right? OK.
Now I make-ik skay-tzz? You skay-tk wiz ozzer girl.
You mean me and Rocky? You're watching us?
I can make-ik. You want?
I want.

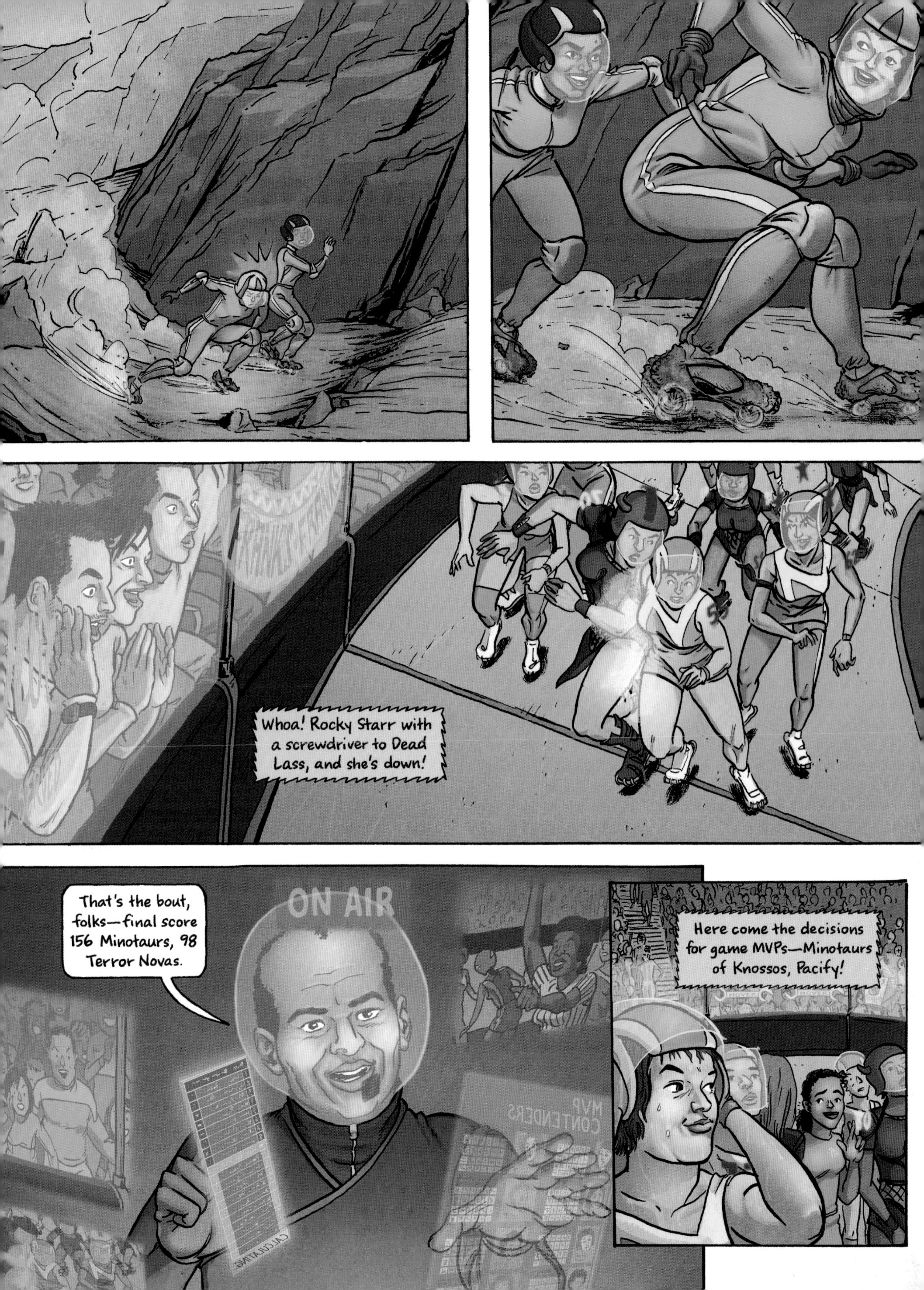
Whoa! Rocky Starr with a screwdriver to Dead Lass, and she's down!
That's the bout, folks—final score 156 Minotaurs, 98 Terror Novas.
ON AIR
Here come the decisions for game MVPs—Minotaurs of Knossos, Pacify!

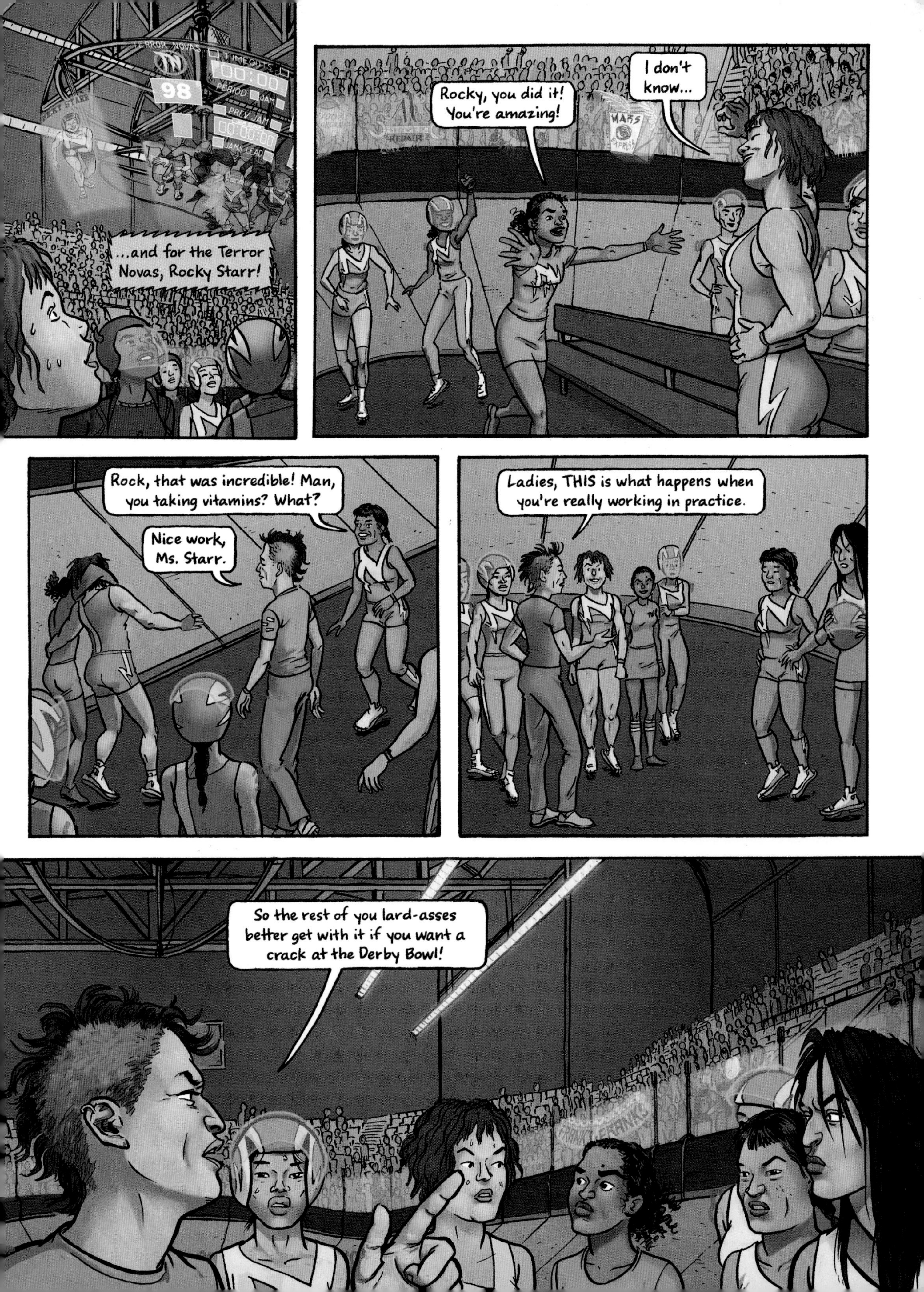
TERROR NOVAS
TIMEOUTS
00:00
98
PERIOD
JAM
PREV JAM
00:00:00
JAMS LEAD
ROCKY STARR
...and for the Terror Novas, Rocky Starr!
Rocky, you did it! You're amazing!
I don't know...
MARS EXPRESS
REPAIR
Rock, that was incredible! Man, you taking vitamins? What?
Nice work, Ms. Starr.
Ladies, THIS is what happens when you're really working in practice.
So the rest of you lard-asses better get with it if you want a crack at the Derby Bowl!
FRANK'S

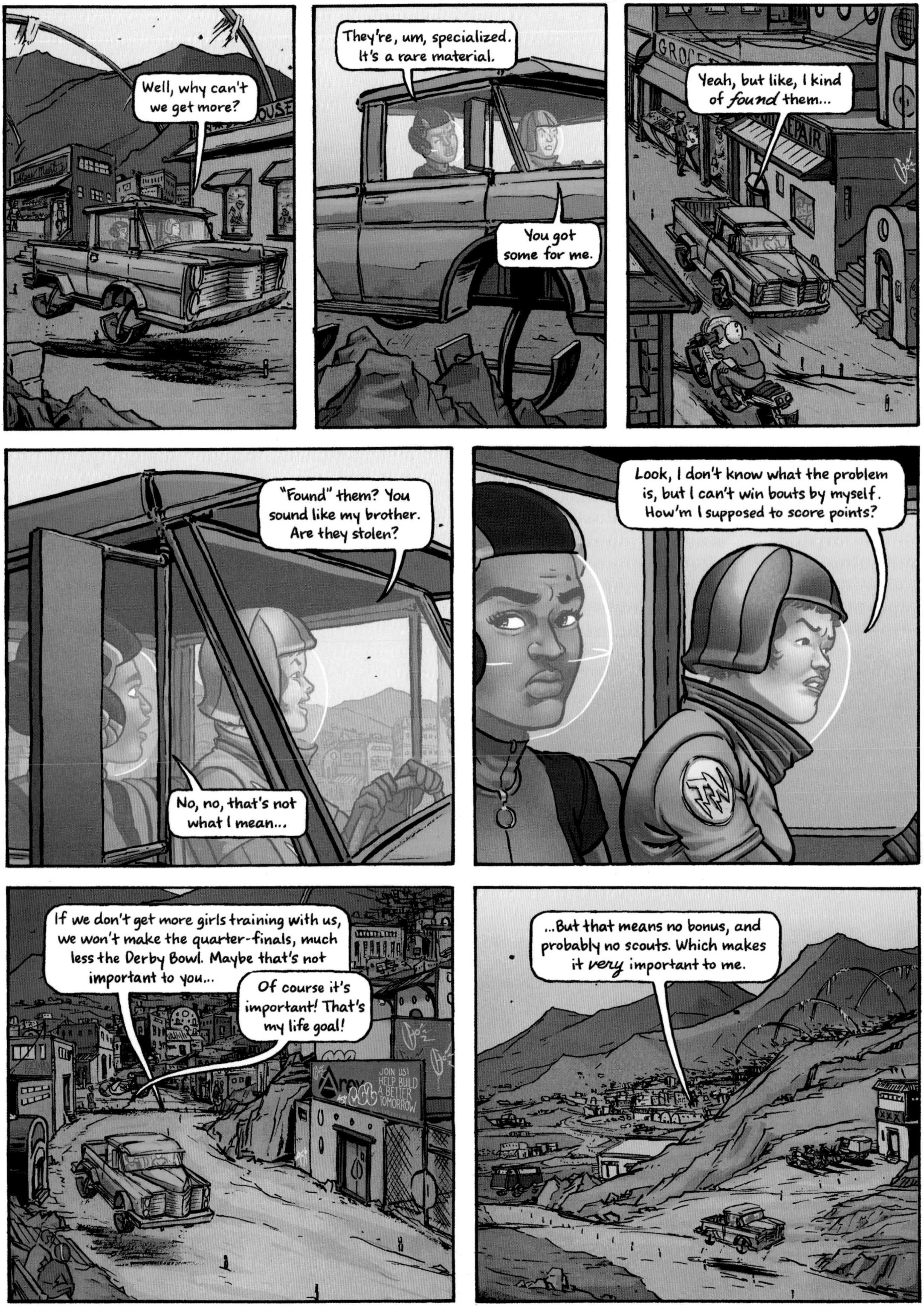
Well, why can't we get more?
They're, um, specialized. It's a rare material.
You got some for me.
Yeah, but like, I kind of *found* them...
REPAIR
"Found" them? You sound like my brother. Are they stolen?
No, no, that's not what I mean...
Look, I don't know what the problem is, but I can't win bouts by myself. How'm I supposed to score points?
If we don't get more girls training with us, we won't make the quarter-finals, much less the Derby Bowl. Maybe that's not important to you...
Of course it's important! That's my life goal!
JOIN US! HELP BUILD A BETTER TOMORROW
...But that means no bonus, and probably no scouts. Which makes it *very* important to me.

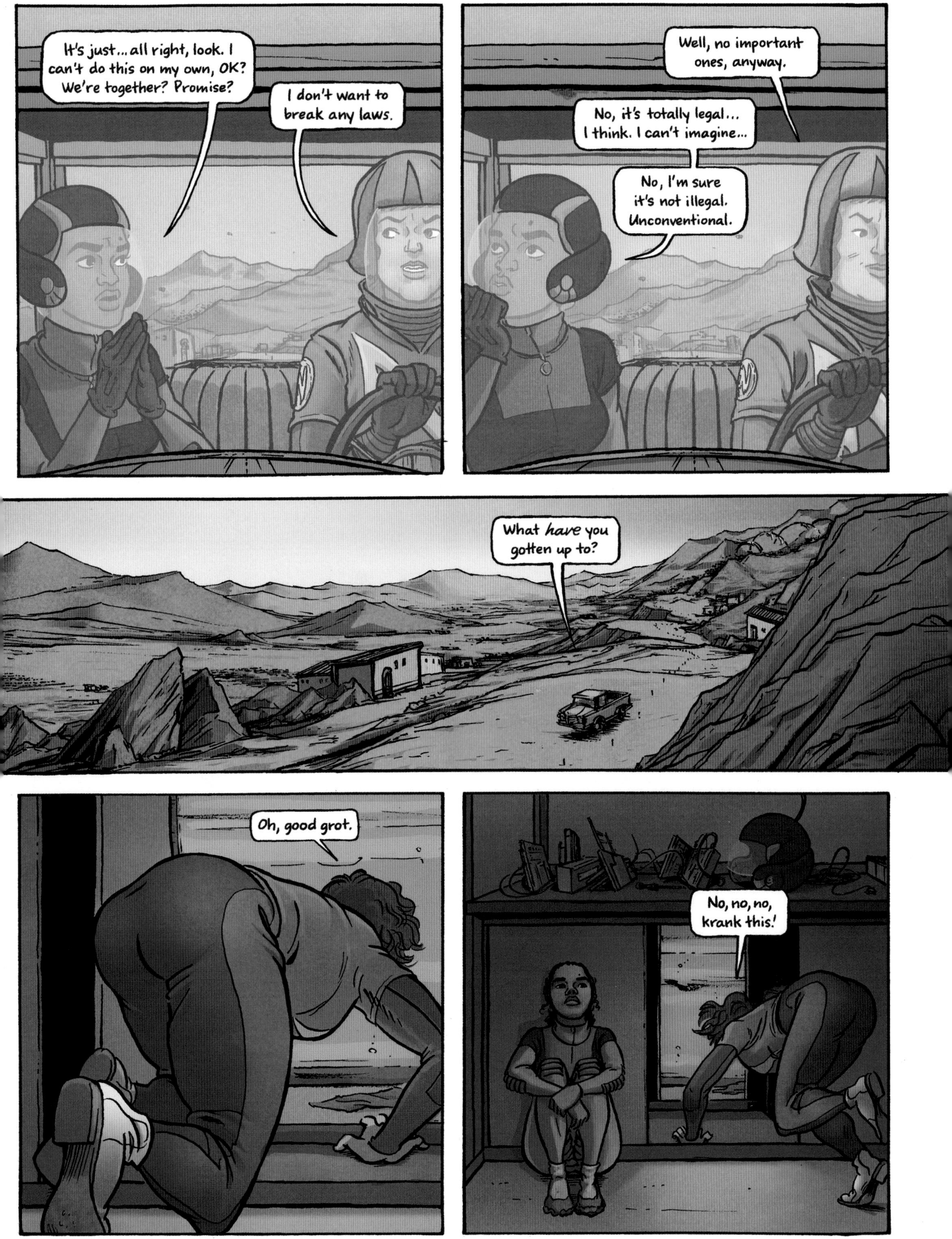
It's just... all right, look. I can't do this on my own, OK? We're together? Promise?
I don't want to break any laws.
No, it's totally legal... I think. I can't imagine...
No, I'm sure it's not illegal. Unconventional.
Well, no important ones, anyway.
What *have* you gotten up to?
Oh, good grot.
No, no, no, krank this!

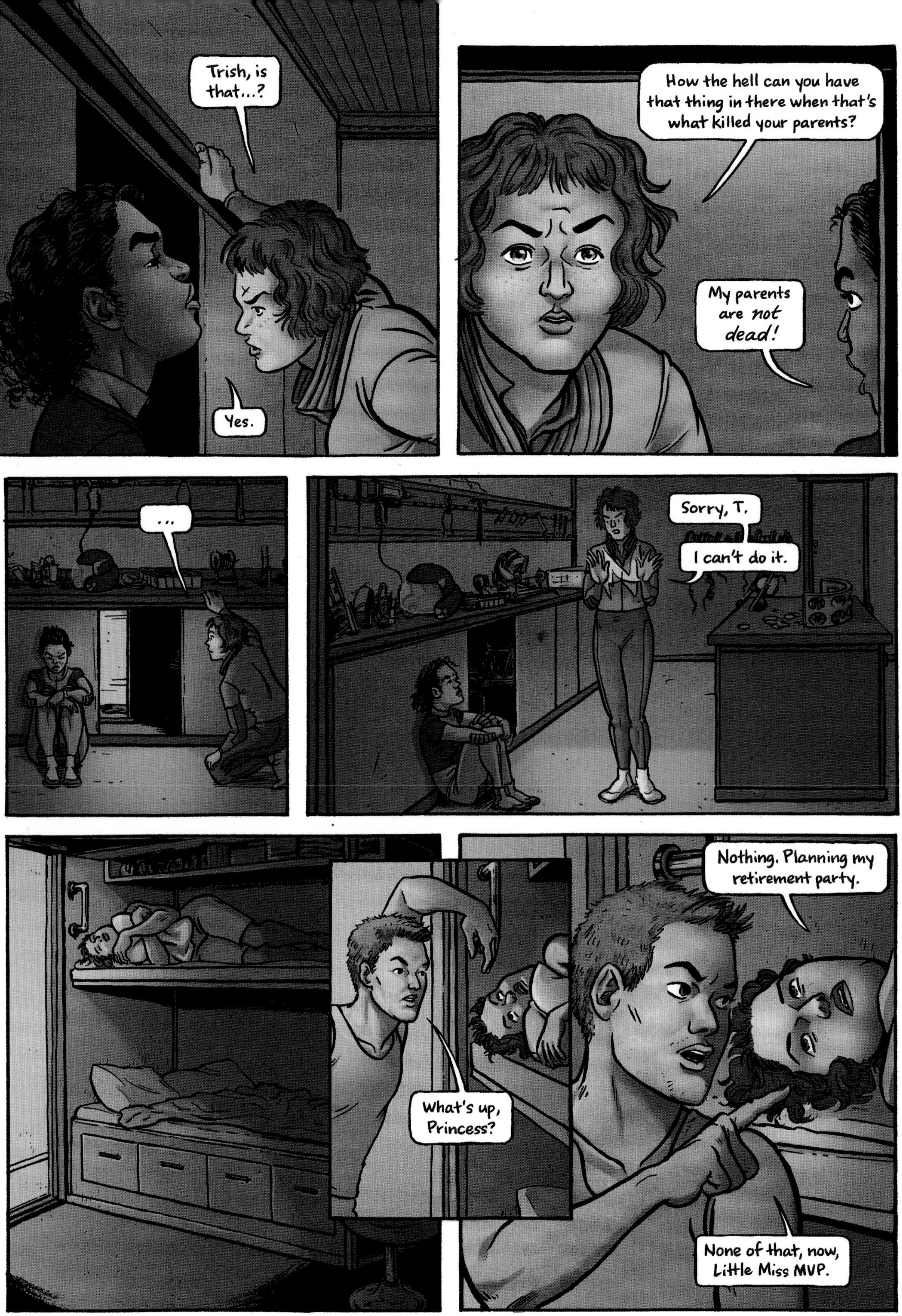

Trish, is that...?
Yes.
How the hell can you have that thing in there when that's what killed your parents?
My parents are not dead!
...
Sorry, T.
I can't do it.
What's up, Princess?
Nothing. Planning my retirement party.
None of that, now, Little Miss MVP.

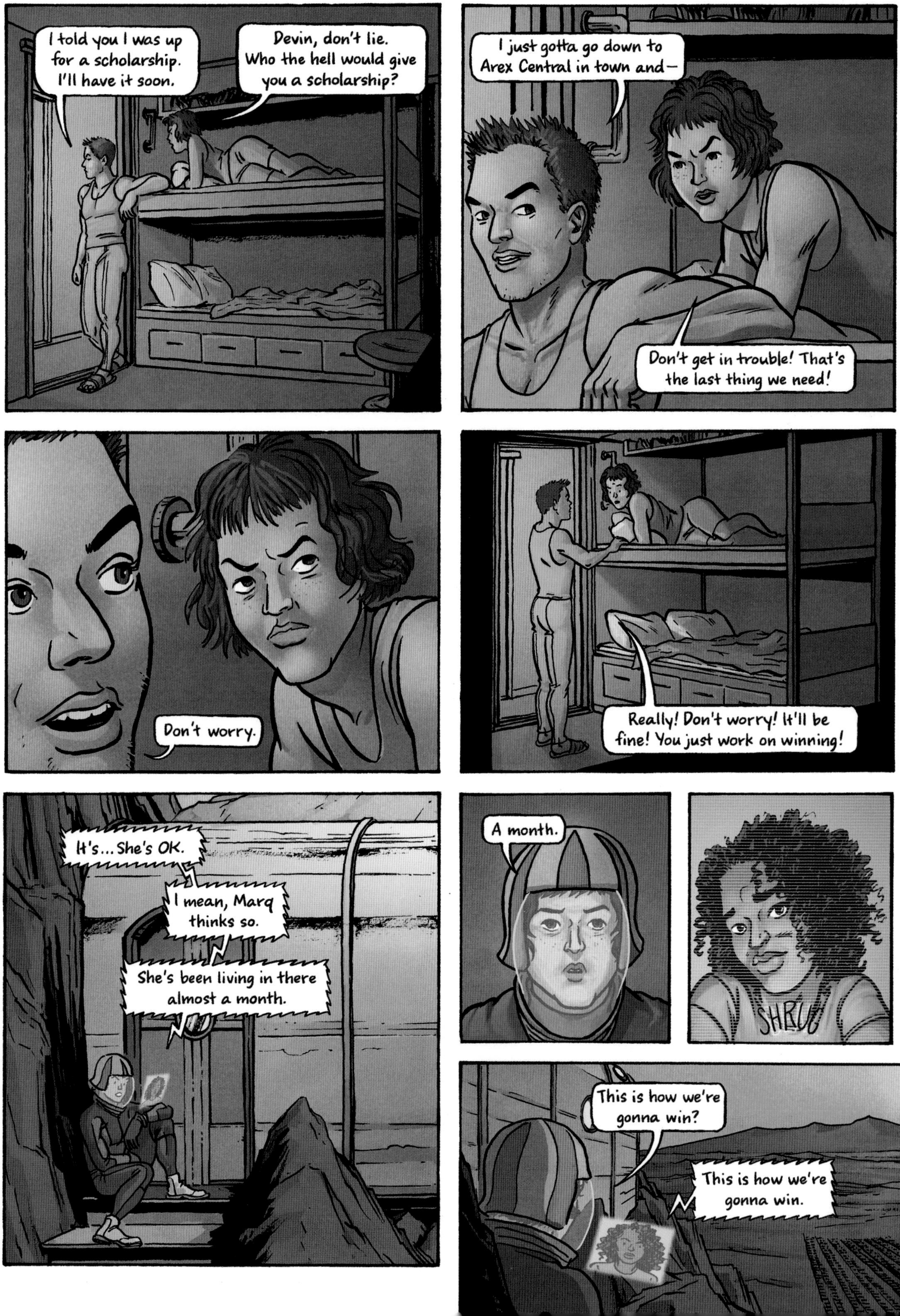
I told you I was up for a scholarship. I'll have it soon.
Devin, don't lie. Who the hell would give you a scholarship?
I just gotta go down to Arex Central in town and—
Don't get in trouble! That's the last thing we need!
Don't worry.
Really! Don't worry! It'll be fine! You just work on winning!
It's... She's OK.
I mean, Marq thinks so.
She's been living in there almost a month.
A month.
SHRUG
This is how we're gonna win?
This is how we're gonna win.

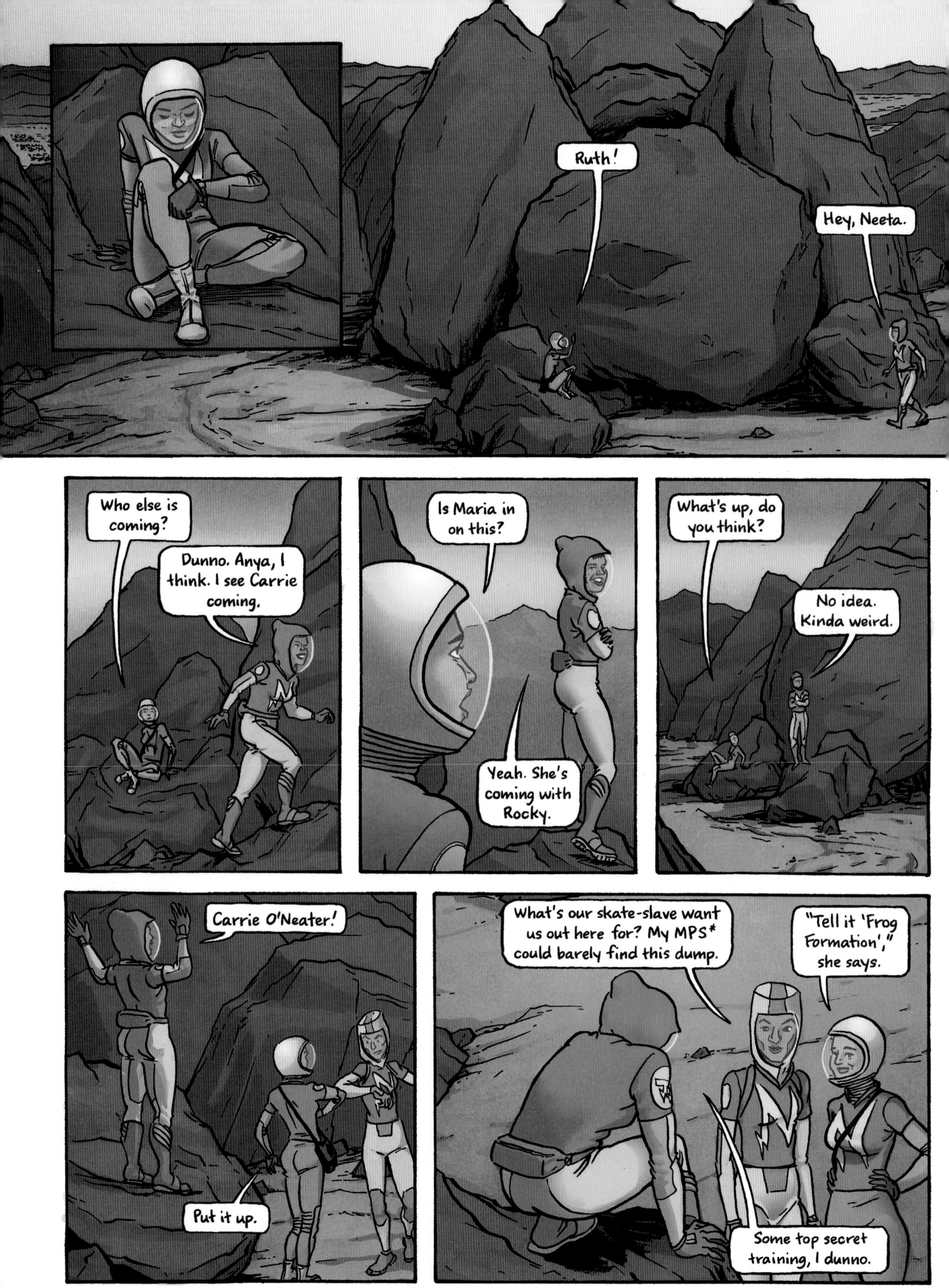
Ruth!
Hey, Neeta.
Who else is coming?
Dunno. Anya, I think. I see Carrie coming.
Is Maria in on this?
Yeah. She's coming with Rocky.
What's up, do you think?
No idea. Kinda weird.
Carrie O'Neater!
Put it up.
What's our skate-slave want us out here for? My MPS* could barely find this dump.
"Tell it 'Frog Formation'," she says.
Some top secret training, I dunno.

* Martian Positioning System

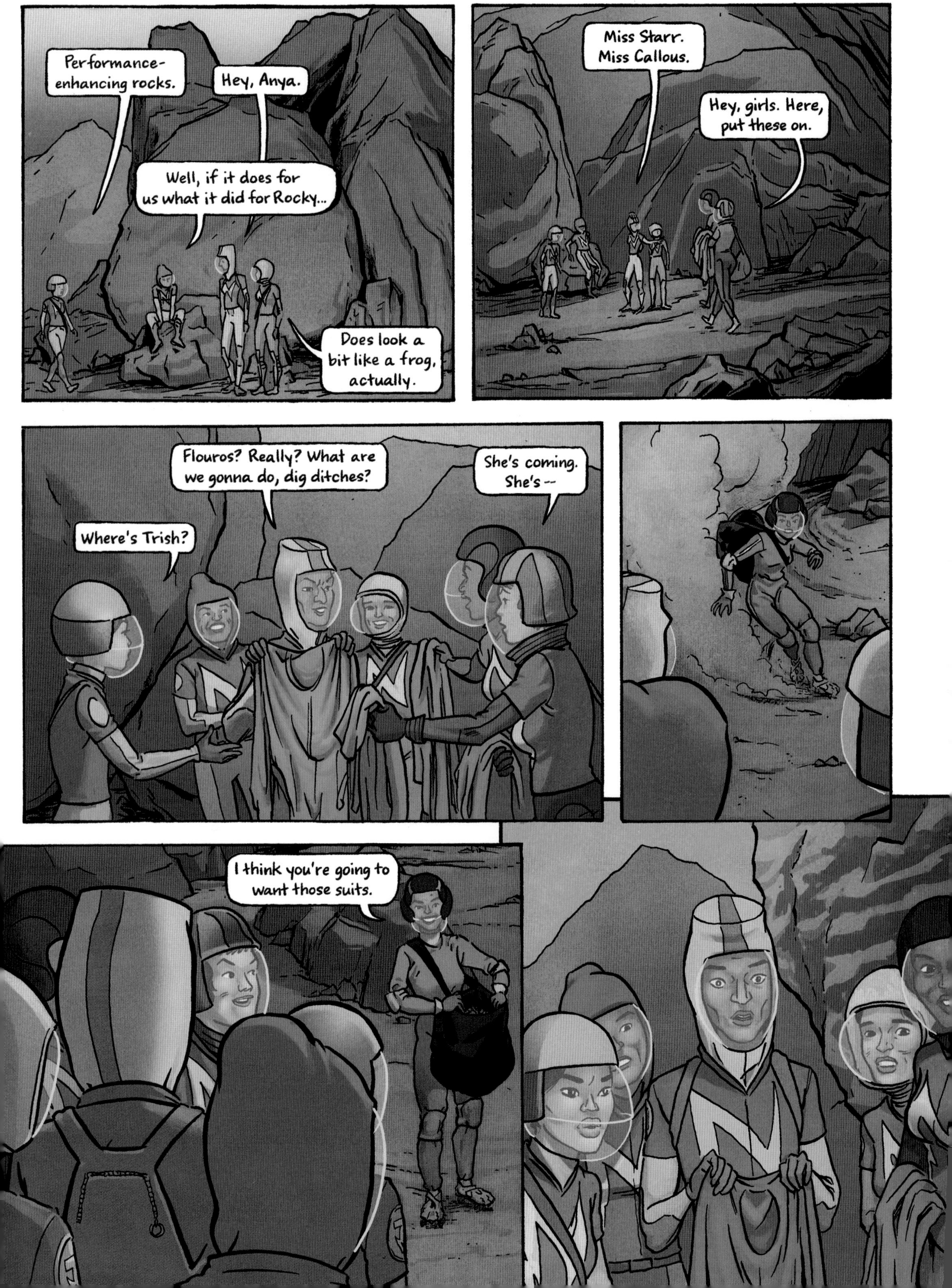

Performance-enhancing rocks.
Hey, Anya.
Well, if it does for us what it did for Rocky...
Does look a bit like a frog, actually.
Miss Starr. Miss Callous.
Hey, girls. Here, put these on.
Where's Trish?
Flouros? Really? What are we gonna do, dig ditches?
She's coming. She's --
I think you're going to want those suits.

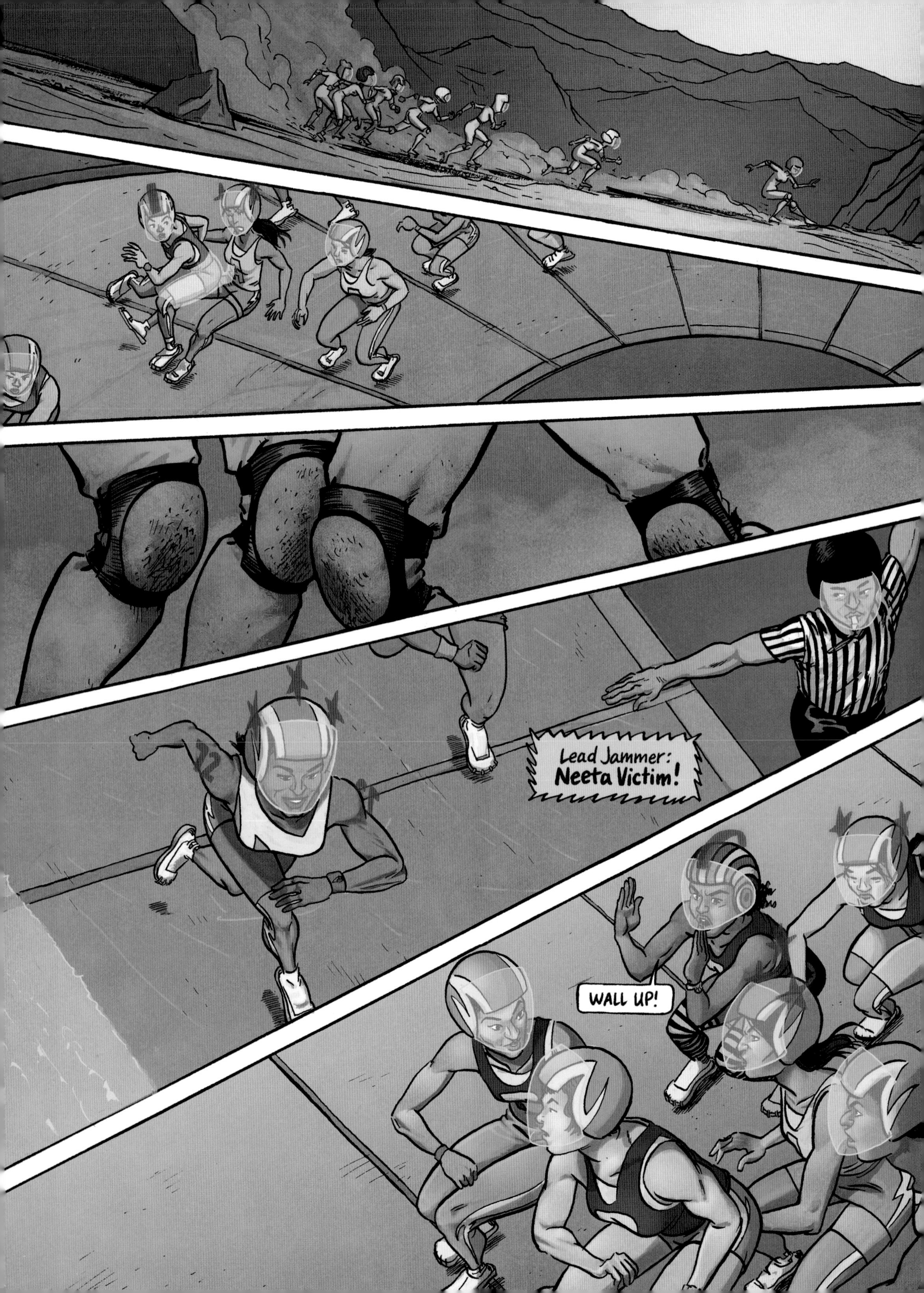
Lead Jammer:
Neeta Victim!
WALL UP!

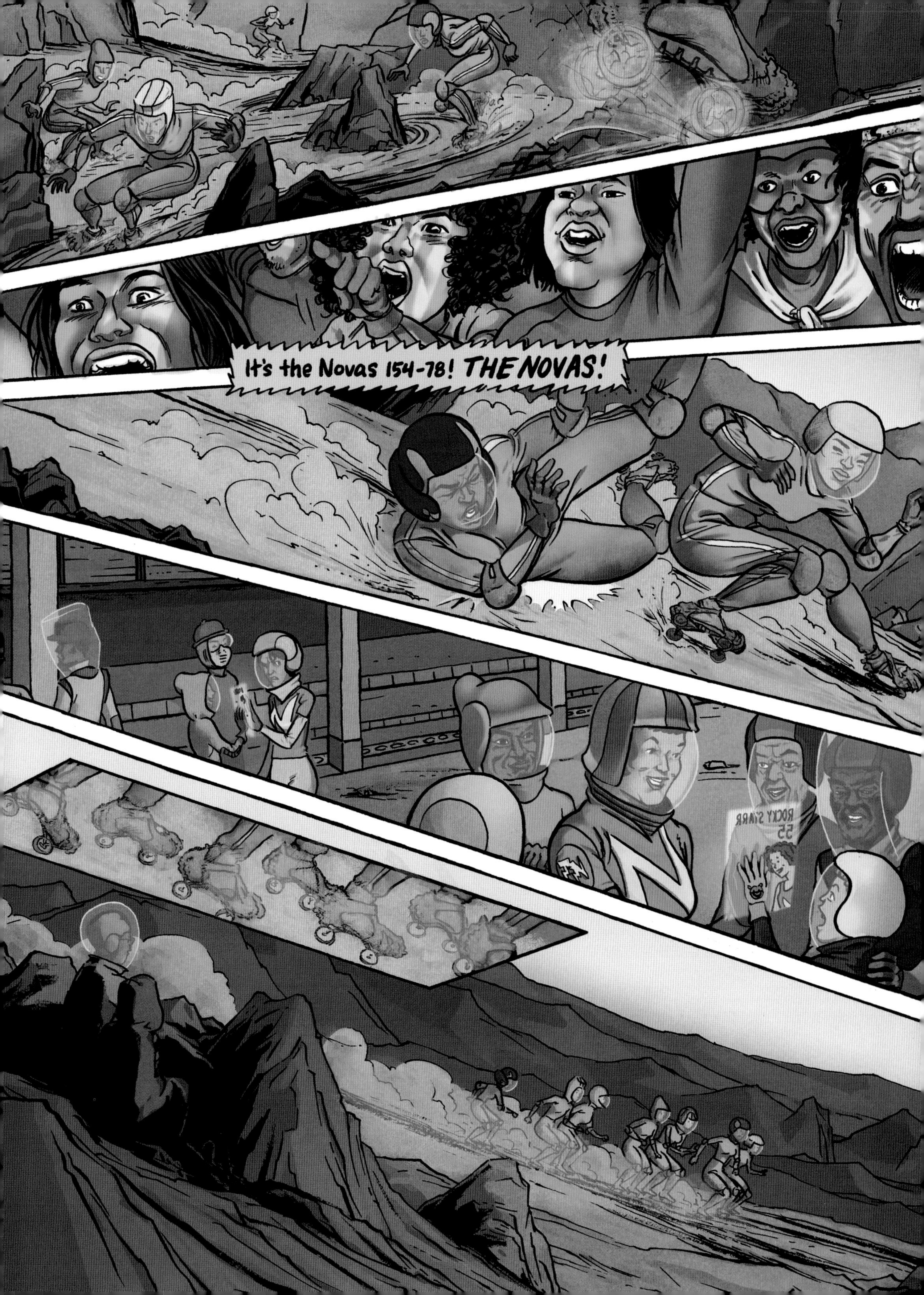
It's the Novas 154-78! THE NOVAS!
ROCKY STARR
55

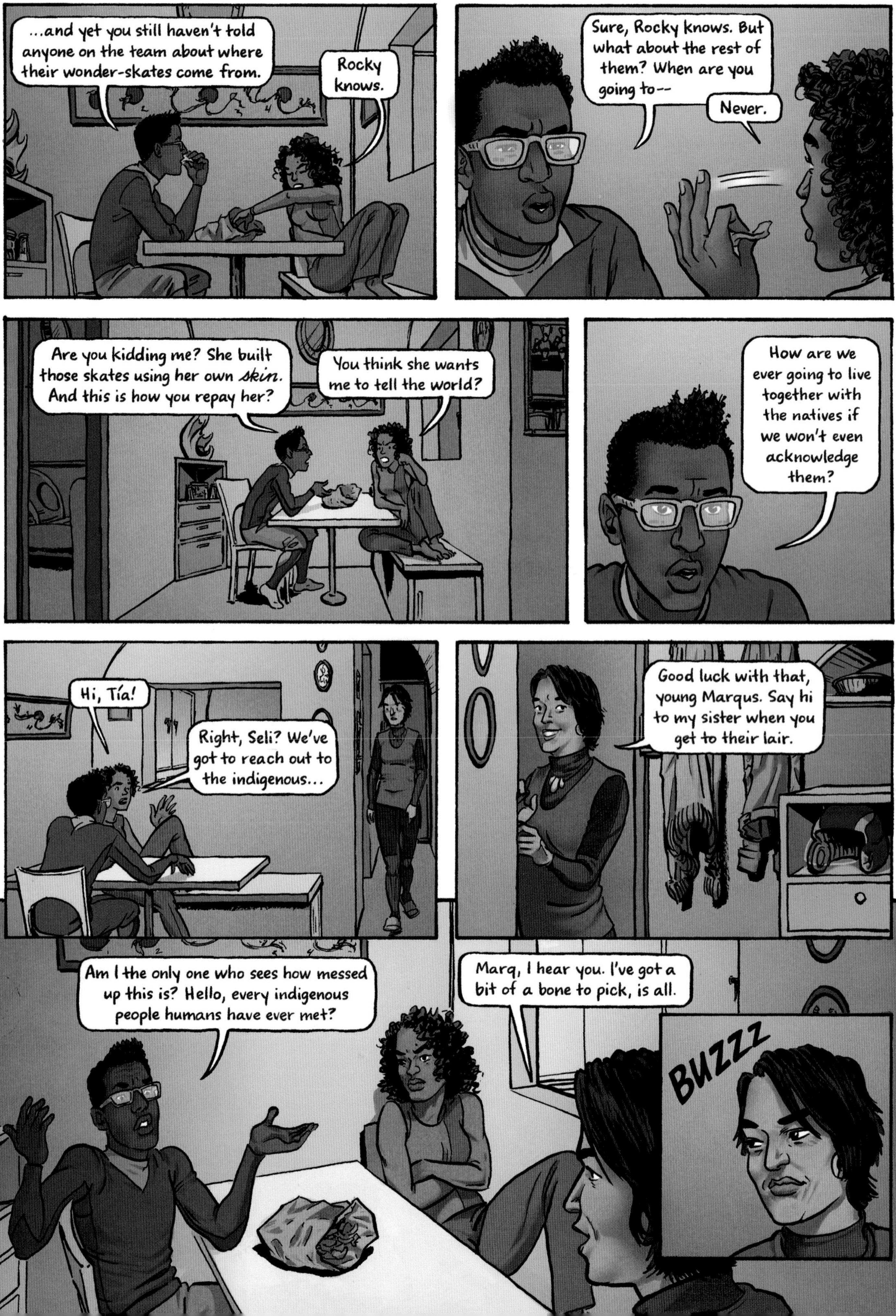
...and yet you still haven't told anyone on the team about where their wonder-skates come from.
Rocky knows.
Sure, Rocky knows. But what about the rest of them? When are you going to--
Never.
Are you kidding me? She built those skates using her own *skin*. And this is how you repay her?
You think she wants me to tell the world?
How are we ever going to live together with the natives if we won't even acknowledge them?
Hi, Tía!
Right, Seli? We've got to reach out to the indigenous...
Good luck with that, young Marqus. Say hi to my sister when you get to their lair.
Am I the only one who sees how messed up this is? Hello, every indigenous people humans have ever met?
Marq, I hear you. I've got a bit of a bone to pick, is all.
BUZZZ

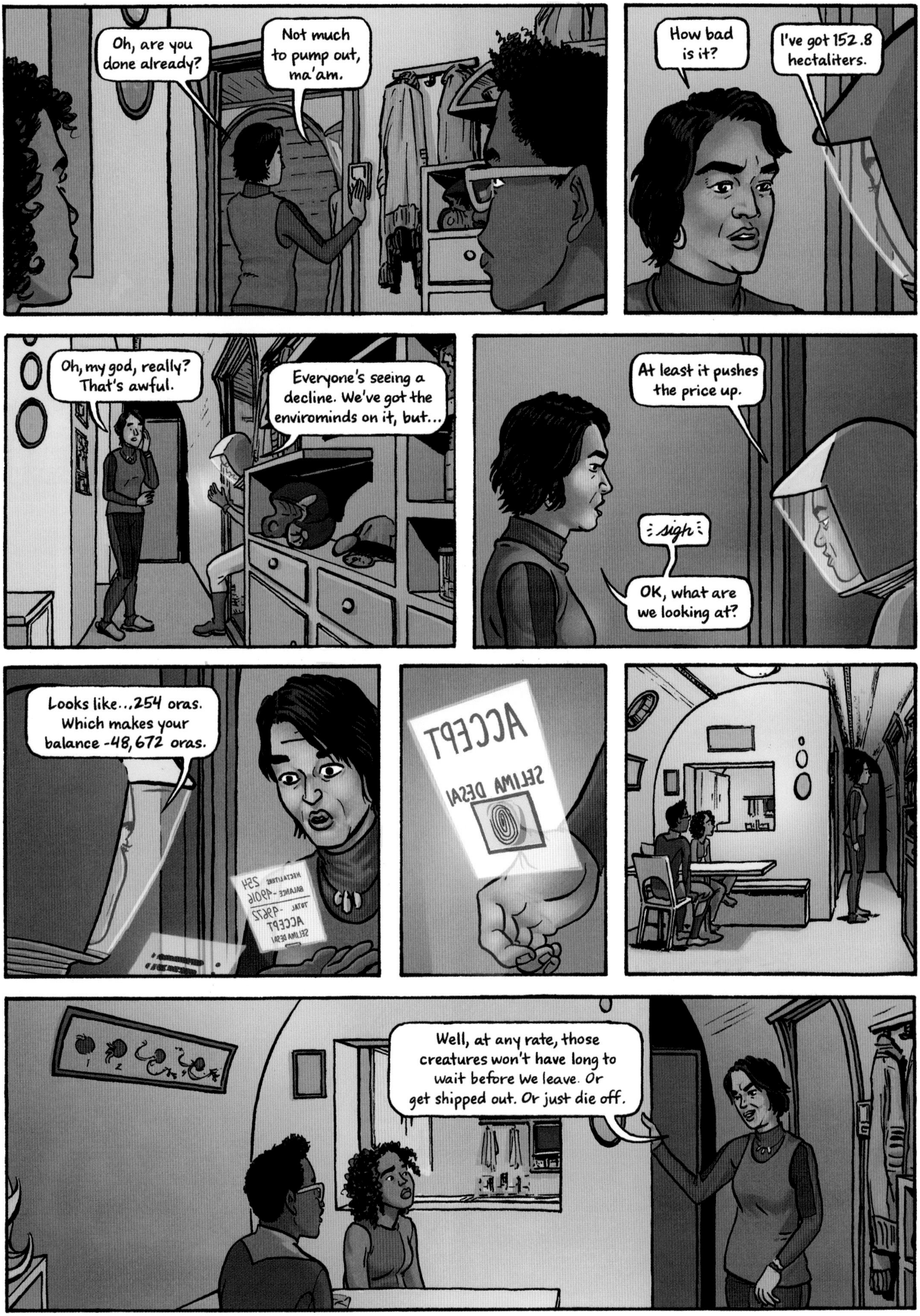

Oh, are you done already?
Not much to pump out, ma'am.
How bad is it?
I've got 152.8 hectaliters.
Oh, my god, really? That's awful.
Everyone's seeing a decline. We've got the envirominds on it, but...
At least it pushes the price up.
sigh
OK, what are we looking at?
Looks like...254 oras. Which makes your balance -48,672 oras.
ACCEPT
SELIMA DESAI
Well, at any rate, those creatures won't have long to wait before we leave. Or get shipped out. Or just die off.

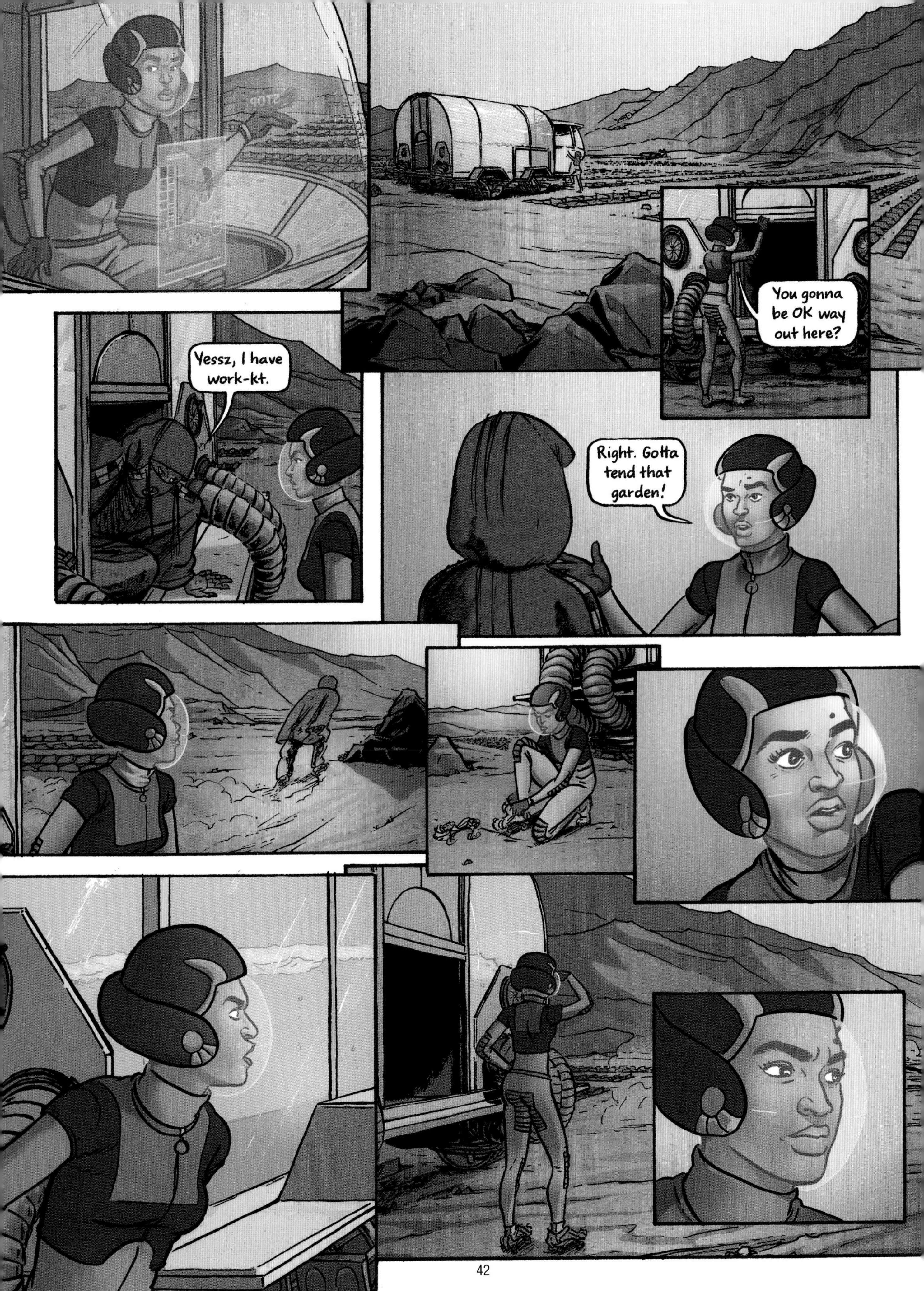
STOP
You gonna be OK way out here?
Yessz, I have work-kt.
Right. Gotta tend that garden!

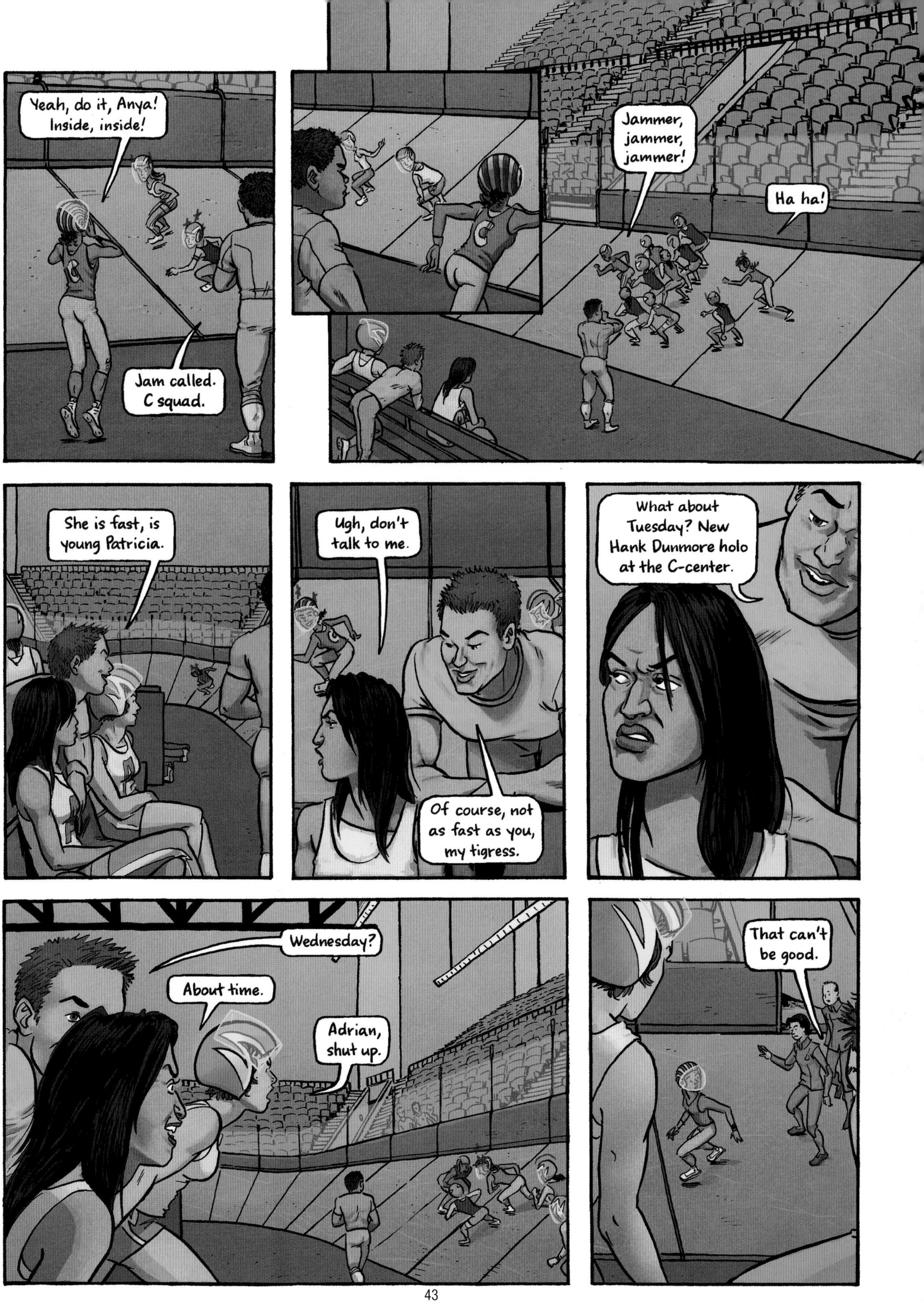
Yeah, do it, Anya! Inside, inside!
Jam called. C squad.
Jammer, jammer, jammer!
Ha ha!
She is fast, is young Patricia.
Ugh, don't talk to me.
Of course, not as fast as you, my tigress.
What about Tuesday? New Hank Dunmore holo at the C-center.
Wednesday?
About time.
Adrian, shut up.
That can't be good.

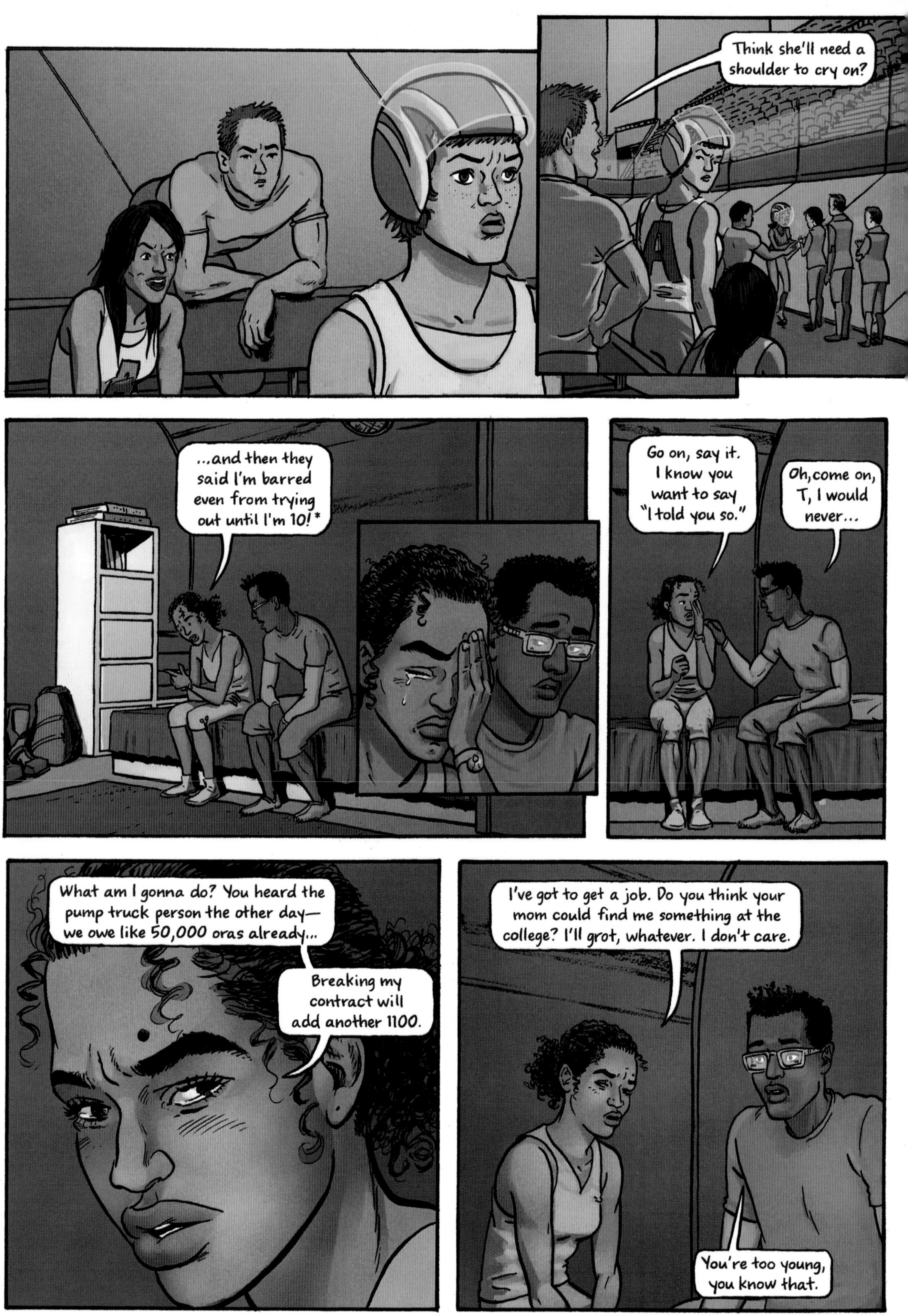
Think she'll need a shoulder to cry on?
...and then they said I'm barred even from trying out until I'm 10!*
Go on, say it. I know you want to say "I told you so."
Oh, come on, T, I would never...
What am I gonna do? You heard the pump truck person the other day—we owe like 50,000 oras already...
Breaking my contract will add another 1100.
I've got to get a job. Do you think your mom could find me something at the college? I'll grot, whatever. I don't care.
You're too young, you know that.

* Twenty in Earth years. Martian years are twice as long as those on Earth.

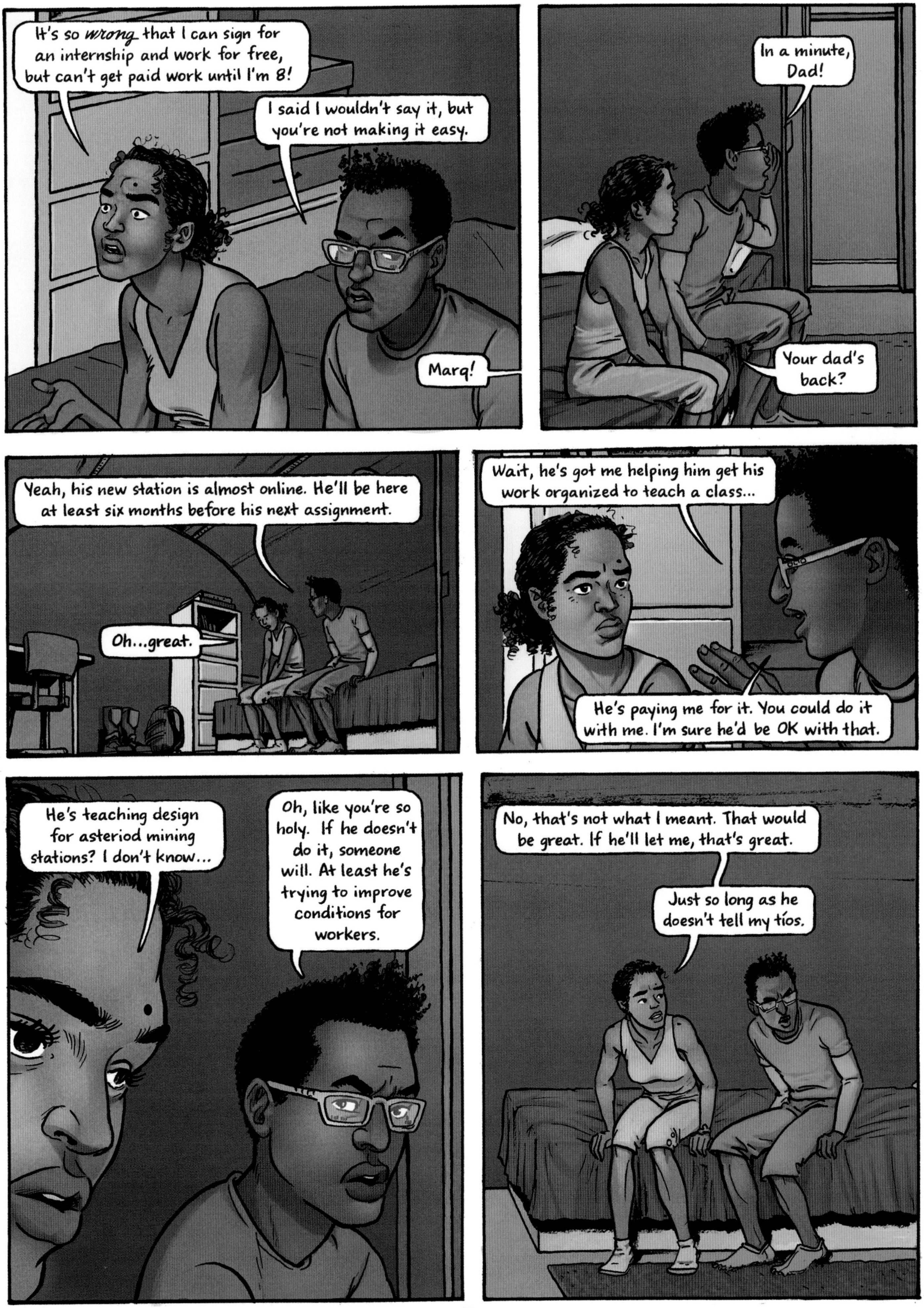

It's so *wrong* that I can sign for an internship and work for free, but can't get paid work until I'm 8!
I said I wouldn't say it, but you're not making it easy.
Marq!
In a minute, Dad!
Your dad's back?
Yeah, his new station is almost online. He'll be here at least six months before his next assignment.
Oh...great.
Wait, he's got me helping him get his work organized to teach a class...
He's paying me for it. You could do it with me. I'm sure he'd be OK with that.
He's teaching design for asteriod mining stations? I don't know...
Oh, like you're so holy. If he doesn't do it, someone will. At least he's trying to improve conditions for workers.
No, that's not what I meant. That would be great. If he'll let me, that's great.
Just so long as he doesn't tell my tíos.

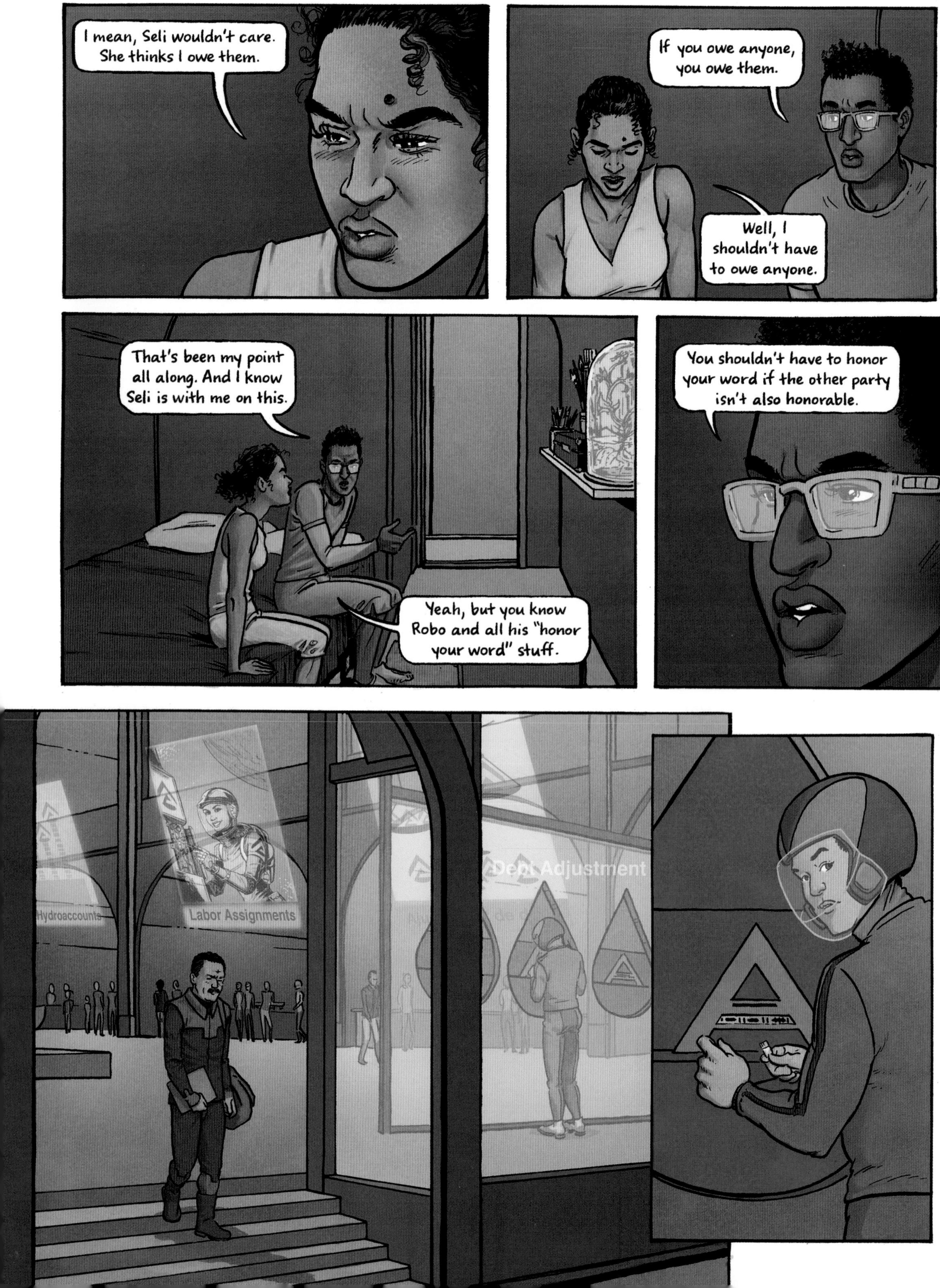
I mean, Seli wouldn't care. She thinks I owe them.
If you owe anyone, you owe them.
Well, I shouldn't have to owe anyone.
That's been my point all along. And I know Seli is with me on this.
Yeah, but you know Robo and all his "honor your word" stuff.
You shouldn't have to honor your word if the other party isn't also honorable.
Hydroaccounts
Labor Assignments
Debt Adjustment

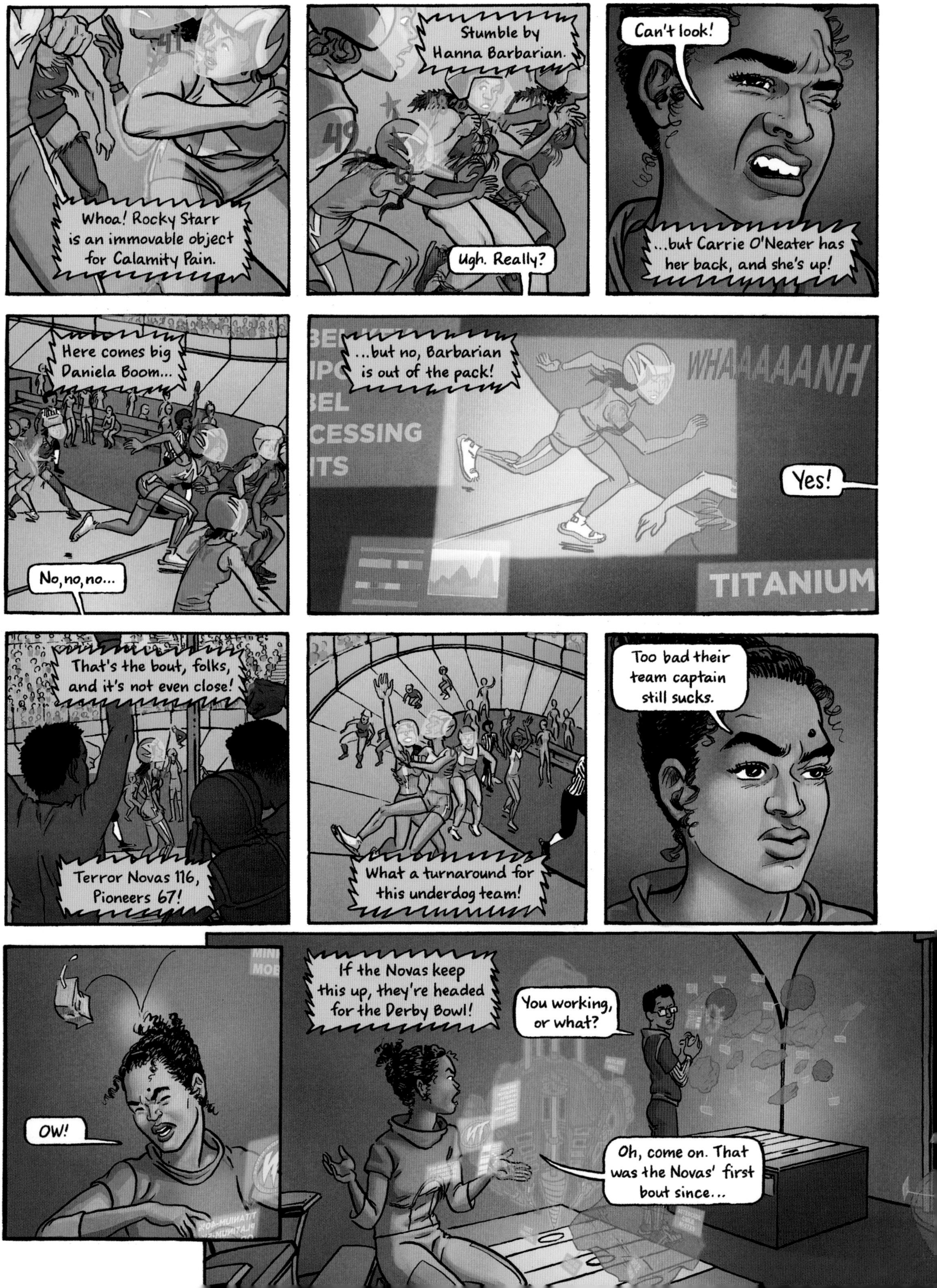
Whoa! Rocky Starr is an immovable object for Calamity Pain.
Stumble by Hanna Barbarian.
Ugh. Really?
Can't look!
...but Carrie O'Neater has her back, and she's up!
Here comes big Daniela Boom...
No, no, no...
...but no, Barbarian is out of the pack!
WHAAAAANH
TITANIUM
Yes!
That's the bout, folks, and it's not even close!
Terror Novas 116, Pioneers 67!
What a turnaround for this underdog team!
Too bad their team captain still sucks.
OW!
If the Novas keep this up, they're headed for the Derby Bowl!
You working, or what?
Oh, come on. That was the Novas' first bout since...

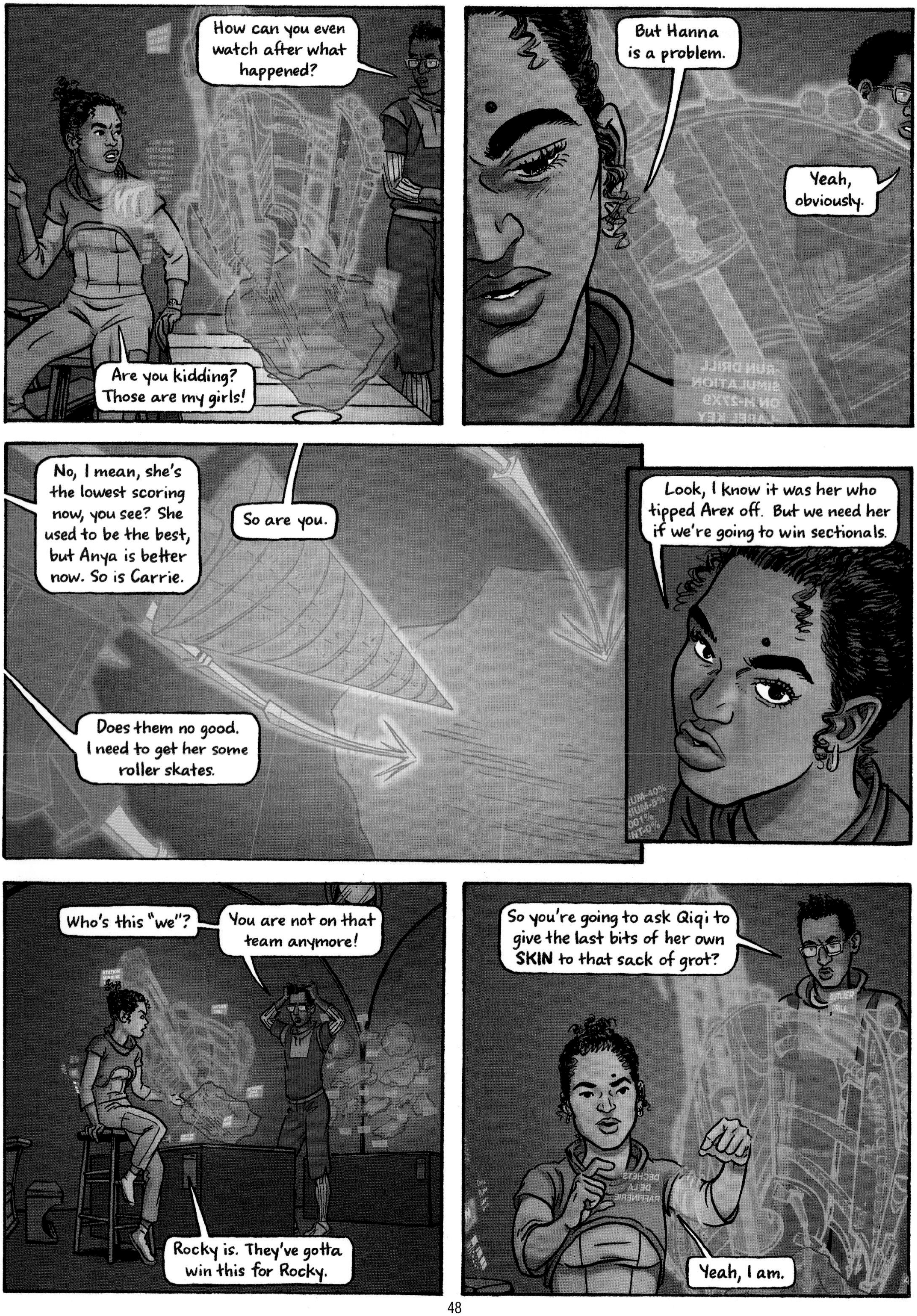
How can you even watch after what happened?
Are you kidding? Those are my girls!
But Hanna is a problem.
Yeah, obviously.
No, I mean, she's the lowest scoring now, you see? She used to be the best, but Anya is better now. So is Carrie.
So are you.
Does them no good. I need to get her some roller skates.
Look, I know it was her who tipped Arex off. But we need her if we're going to win sectionals.
Who's this "we"?
You are not on that team anymore!
Rocky is. They've gotta win this for Rocky.
So you're going to ask Qiqi to give the last bits of her own **SKIN** to that sack of grot?
Yeah, I am.

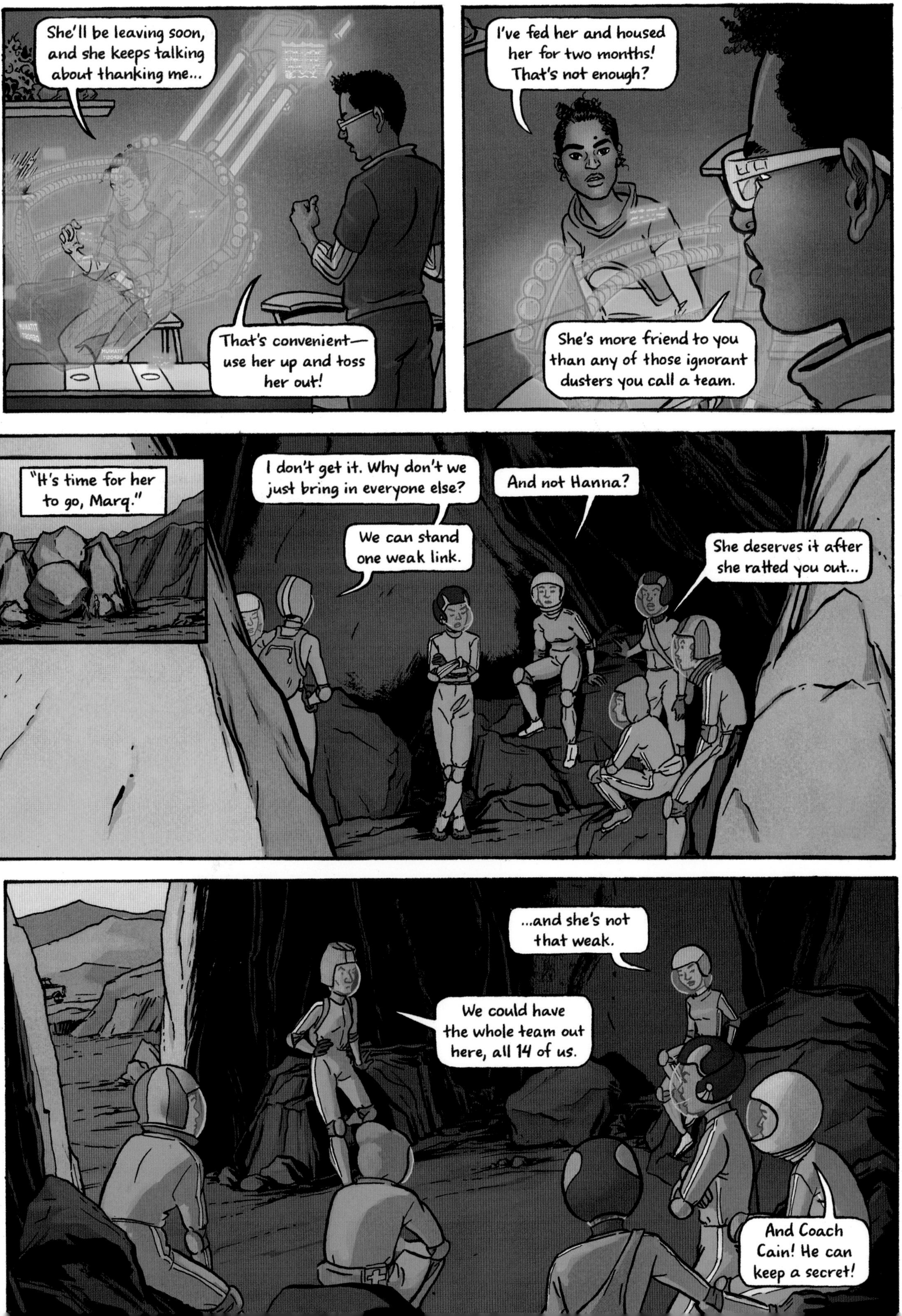
She'll be leaving soon, and she keeps talking about thanking me...
That's convenient—use her up and toss her out!
I've fed her and housed her for two months! That's not enough?
She's more friend to you than any of those ignorant dusters you call a team.
"It's time for her to go, Marq."
I don't get it. Why don't we just bring in everyone else?
We can stand one weak link.
And not Hanna?
She deserves it after she ratted you out...
...and she's not that weak.
We could have the whole team out here, all 14 of us.
And Coach Cain! He can keep a secret!

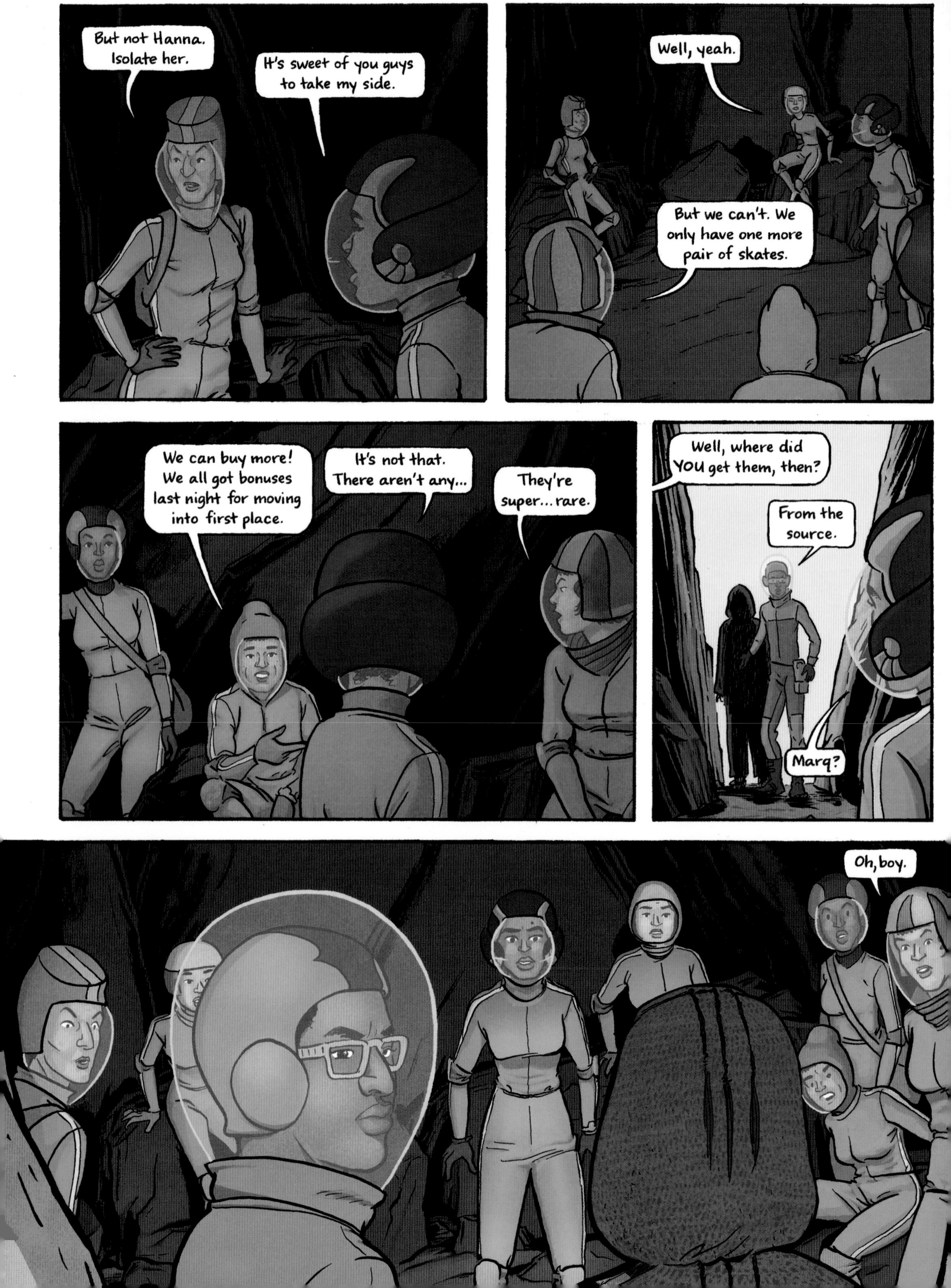
But not Hanna. Isolate her.
It's sweet of you guys to take my side.
Well, yeah.
But we can't. We only have one more pair of skates.
We can buy more! We all got bonuses last night for moving into first place.
It's not that. There aren't any...
They're super... rare.
Well, where did YOU get them, then?
From the source.
Marq?
Oh, boy.

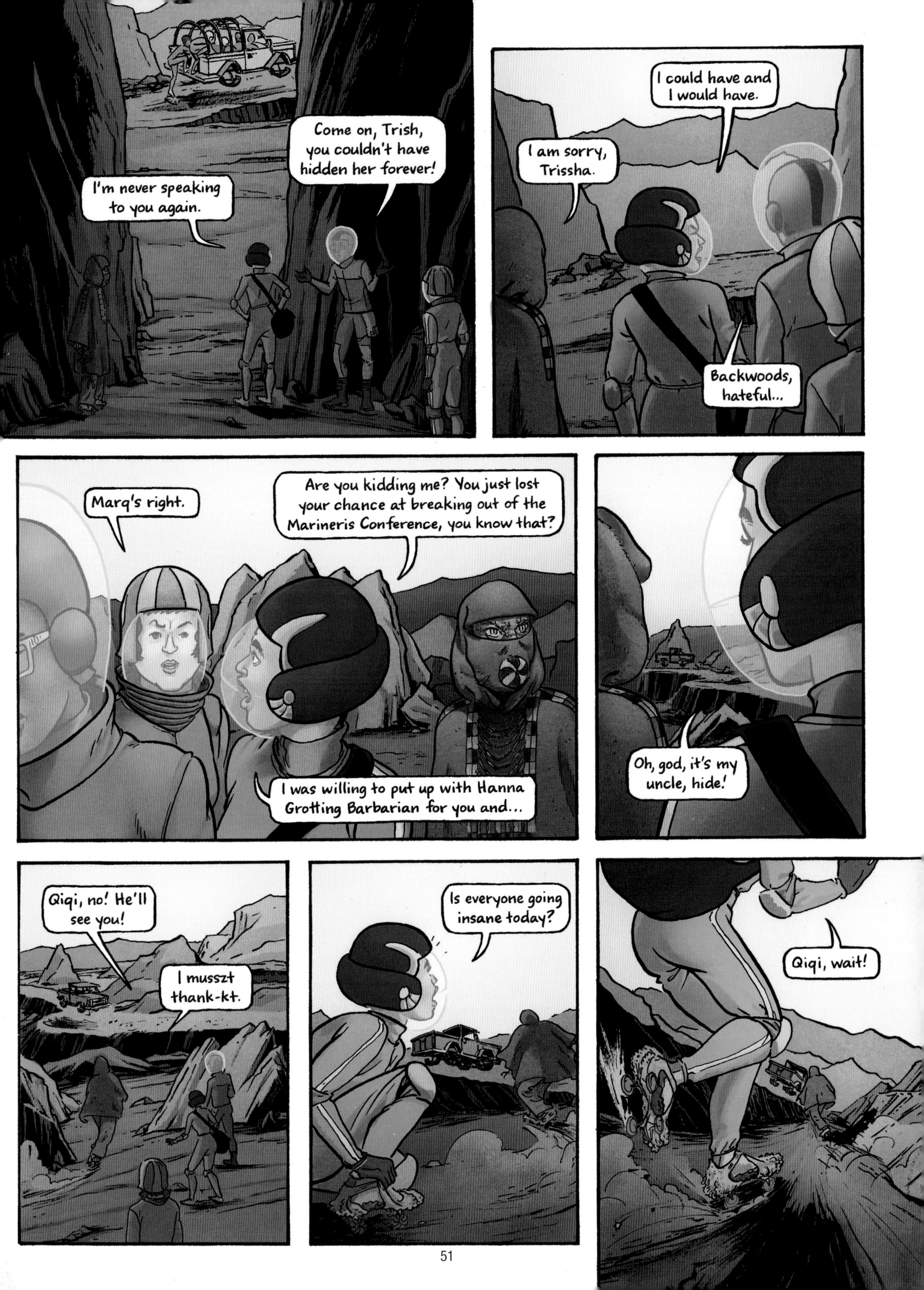
I'm never speaking to you again.
Come on, Trish, you couldn't have hidden her forever!
I am sorry, Trissha.
I could have and I would have.
Backwoods, hateful...
Marq's right.
Are you kidding me? You just lost your chance at breaking out of the Marineris Conference, you know that?
I was willing to put up with Hanna Grotting Barbarian for you and...
Oh, god, it's my uncle, hide!
Qiqi, no! He'll see you!
I musszt thank-kt.
Is everyone going insane today?
Qiqi, wait!

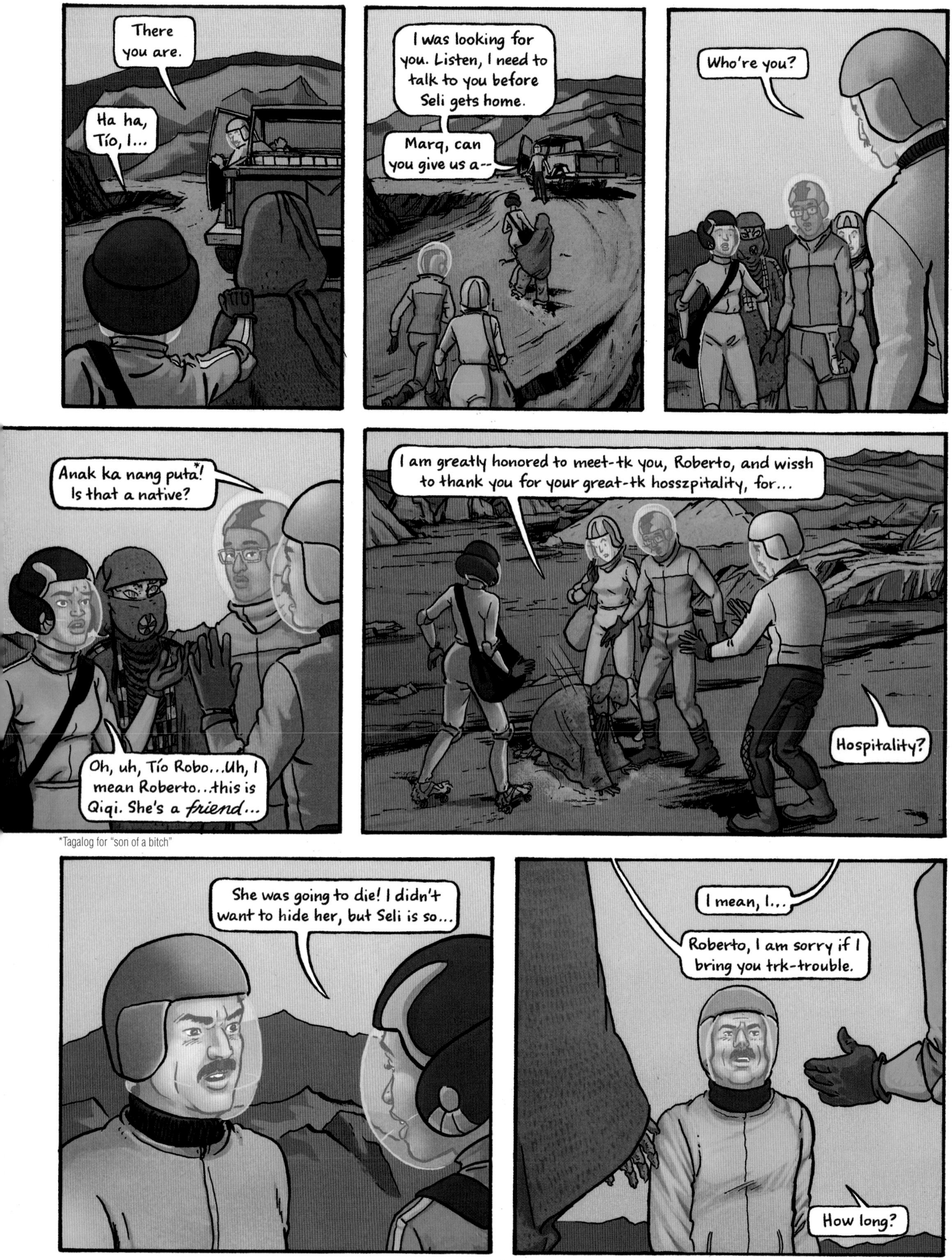
There you are.
Ha ha, Tío, I...
I was looking for you. Listen, I need to talk to you before Seli gets home.
Marq, can you give us a--
Who're you?
Anak ka nang puta!* Is that a native?
Oh, uh, Tío Robo...Uh, I mean Roberto...this is Qiqi. She's a *friend*...
I am greatly honored to meet-tk you, Roberto, and wissh to thank you for your great-tk hosszpitality, for...
Hospitality?
She was going to die! I didn't want to hide her, but Seli is so...
I mean, I...
Roberto, I am sorry if I bring you trk-trouble.
How long?

*Tagalog for "son of a bitch"

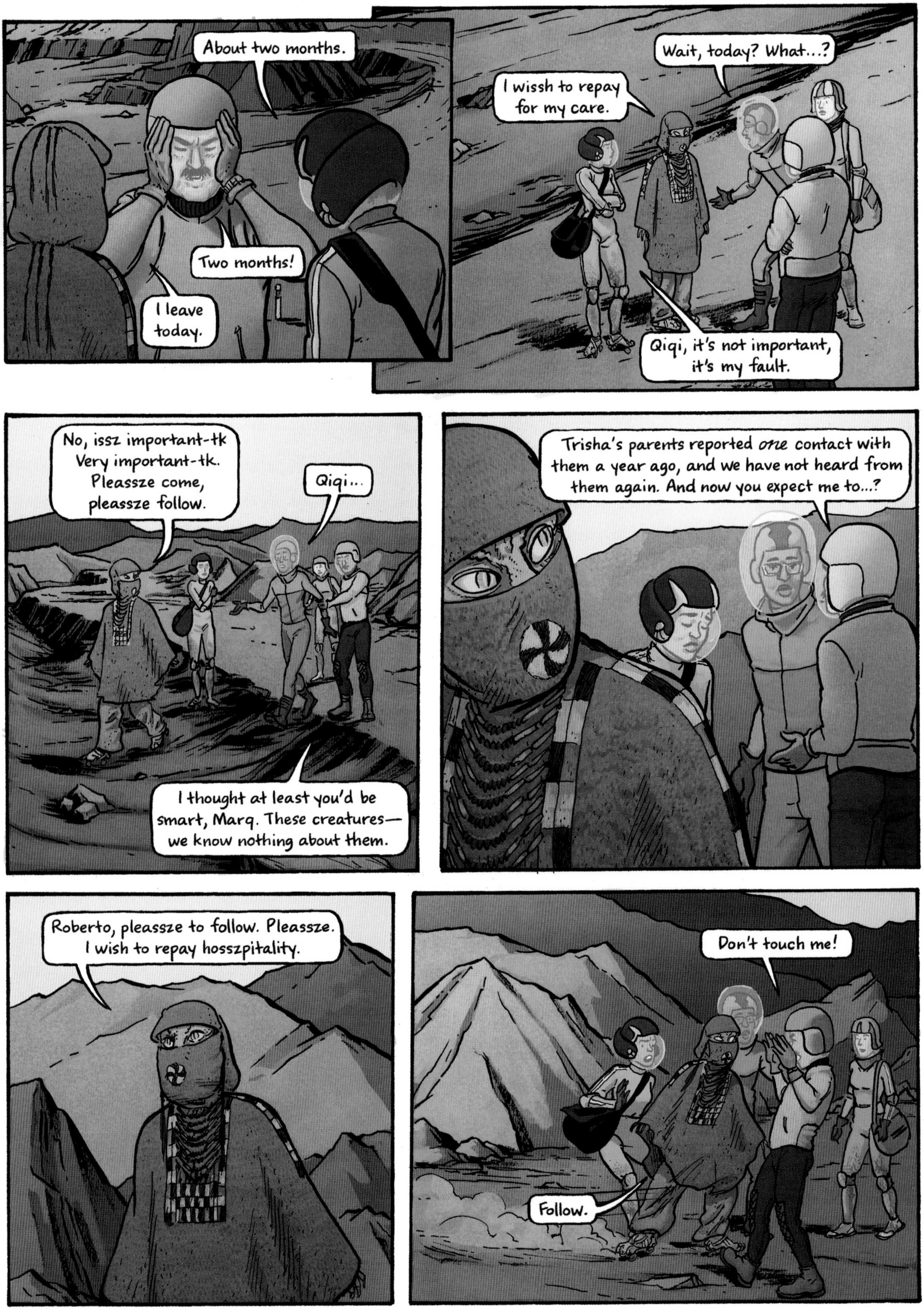
About two months.
Two months!
I leave today.
I wissh to repay for my care.
Wait, today? What...?
Qiqi, it's not important, it's my fault.
No, issz important-tk Very important-tk. Pleassze come, pleassze follow.
Qiqi...
I thought at least you'd be smart, Marq. These creatures— we know nothing about them.
Trisha's parents reported *one* contact with them a year ago, and we have not heard from them again. And now you expect me to...?
Roberto, pleassze to follow. Pleassze. I wish to repay hosszpitality.
Don't touch me!
Follow.

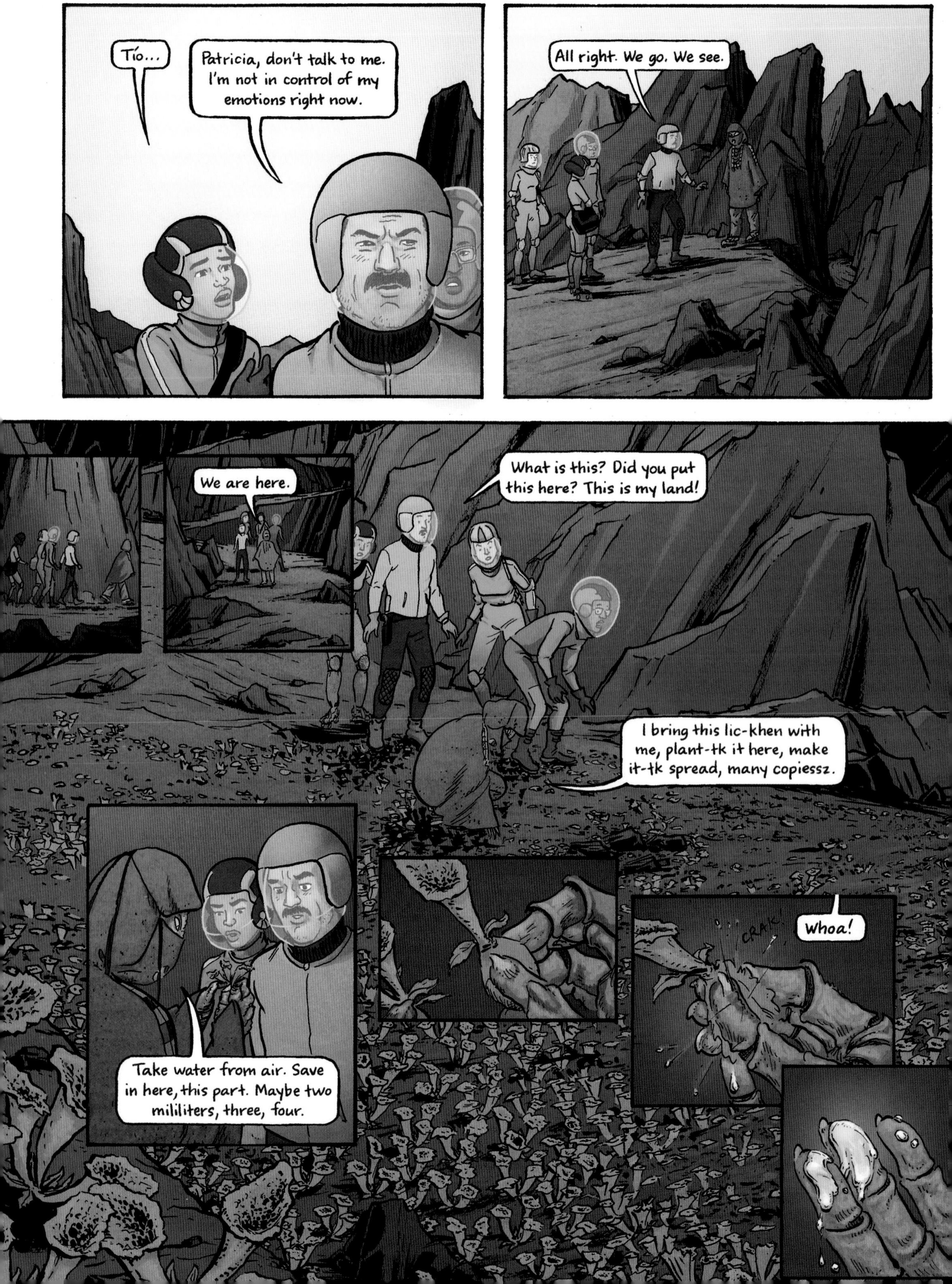
Tío...
Patricia, don't talk to me. I'm not in control of my emotions right now.
All right. We go. We see.
We are here.
What is this? Did you put this here? This is my land!
I bring this lic-khen with me, plant-tk it here, make it-tk spread, many copiessz.
Take water from air. Save in here, this part. Maybe two mililiters, three, four.
CRAK!
Whoa!

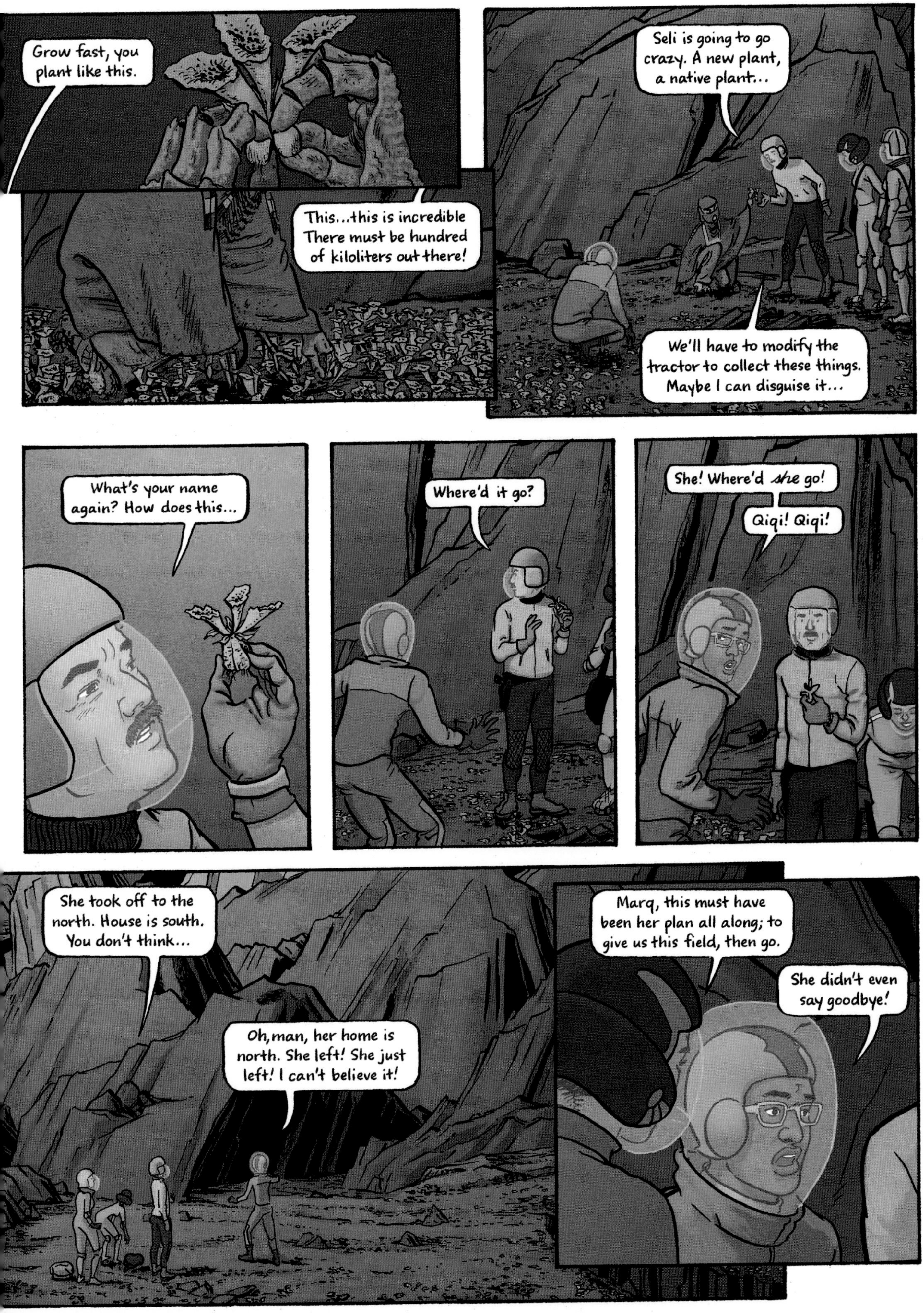
Grow fast, you plant like this.
This...this is incredible There must be hundred of kiloliters out there!
Seli is going to go crazy. A new plant, a native plant...
We'll have to modify the tractor to collect these things. Maybe I can disguise it...
What's your name again? How does this...
Where'd it go?
She! Where'd *she* go!
Qiqi! Qiqi!
She took off to the north. House is south. You don't think...
Oh, man, her home is north. She left! She just left! I can't believe it!
Marq, this must have been her plan all along; to give us this field, then go.
She didn't even say goodbye!

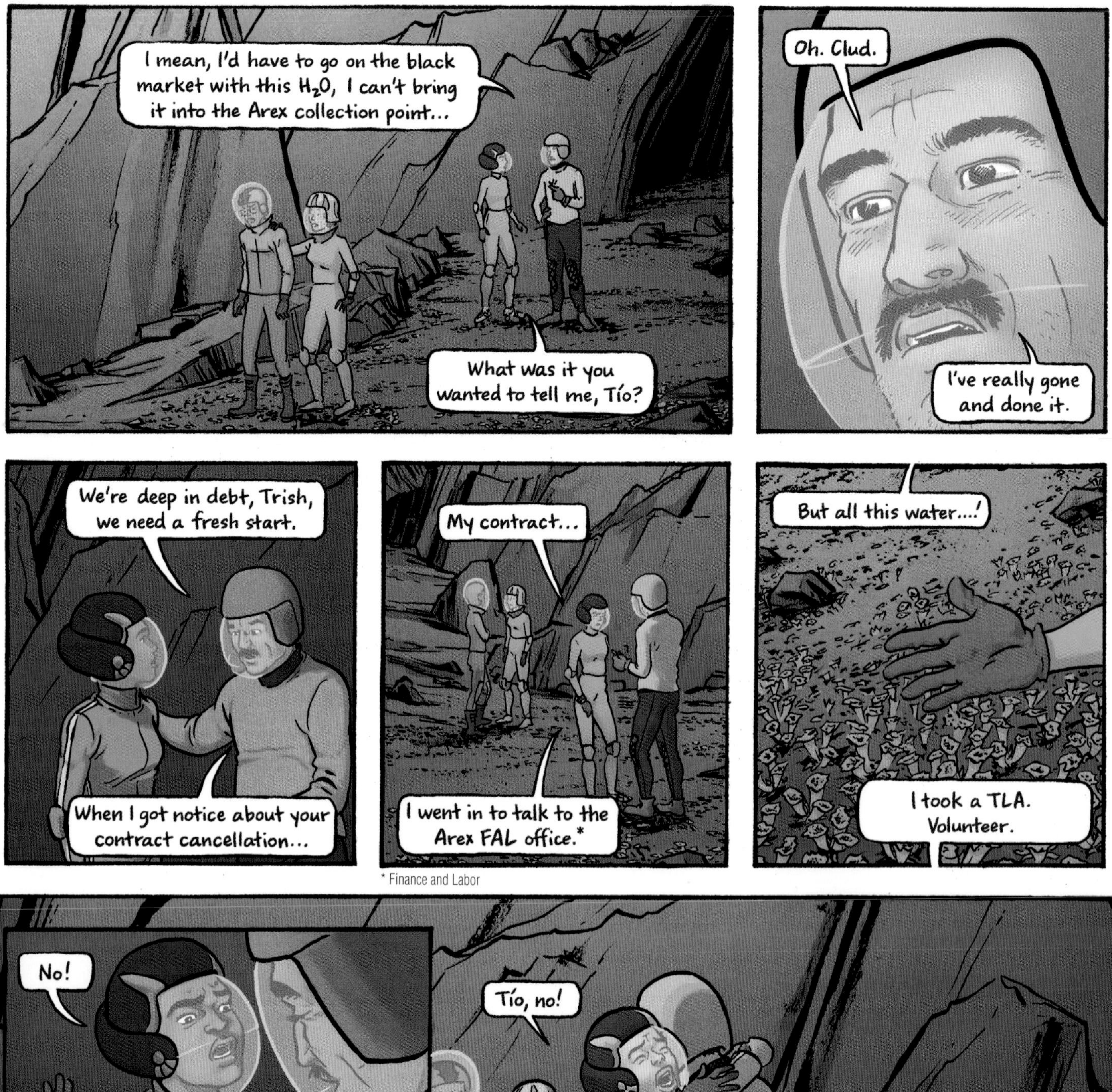
I mean, I'd have to go on the black market with this H_2O, I can't bring it into the Arex collection point...
What was it you wanted to tell me, Tío?
Oh. Clud.
I've really gone and done it.
We're deep in debt, Trish, we need a fresh start.
When I got notice about your contract cancellation...
My contract...
I went in to talk to the Arex FAL office.*
But all this water...!
I took a TLA. Volunteer.

* Finance and Labor

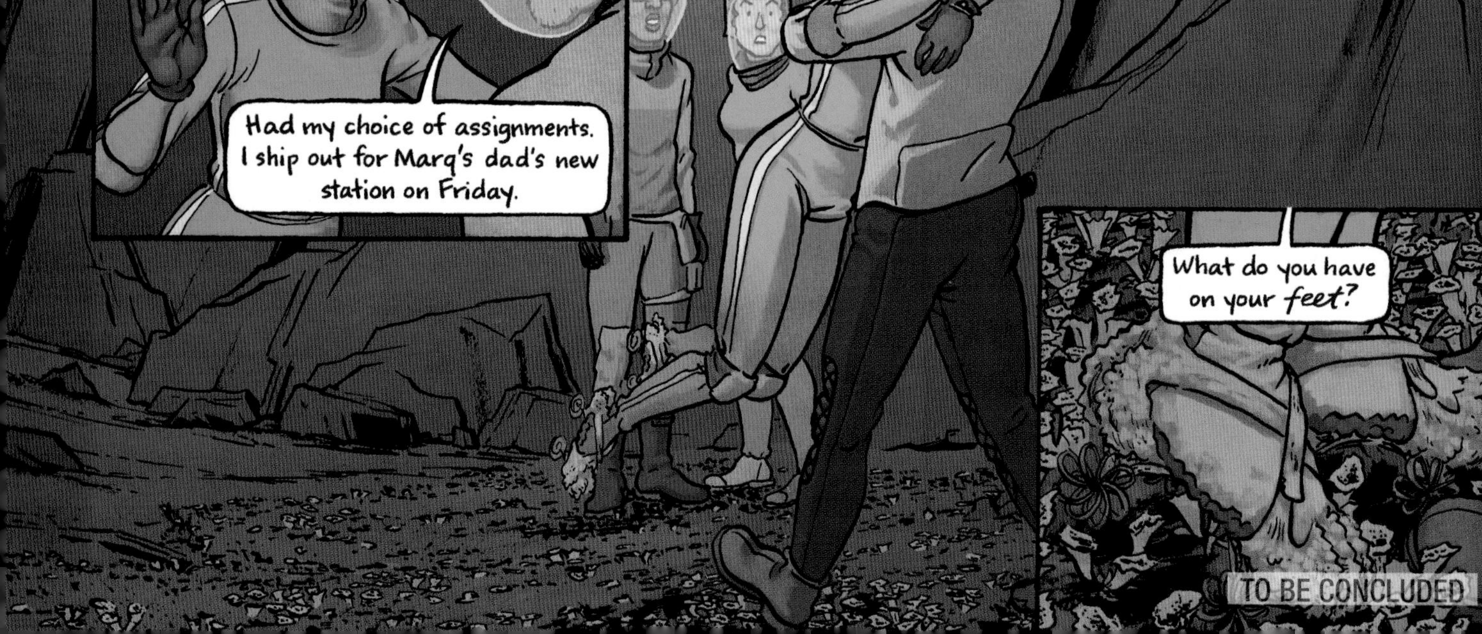
No!
Had my choice of assignments. I ship out for Marq's dad's new station on Friday.
Tío, no!
What do you have on your *feet*?
TO BE CONCLUDED

Ares Collective Statement of Debt (ACSOD) [edit]

The Ares Collective Statement of Debt (ACSOD) is a report run each micro-second on all human Martian residents deriving from their legally-binding contractual obligations with Governmental and Quasi-Governmental Bodies on Mars (GQGBM).

The ACSOD was implemented in ME20 when large numbers of First Wave settlers (Homesteaders) who had signed indenturement contracts for their passage and equipment began to fail and face bankruptcy. Initially, TLAs (Temporary Labor Assignments) were assigned haphazardly and came without warning. The ACSOD was an attempt to standardize application of the TLA Rule and give settlers predictability as to when they might expect to be asked to participate in Civic Labor for the greater good.

The ACSOD can be used to determine eligibility for goods and services provided by the GQGBM, but it is illegal to discriminate based on ACSOD. An individual's ACSOD is instantly accessible to any official of the GQGBM via wristcom, or failing that, retinal scan.

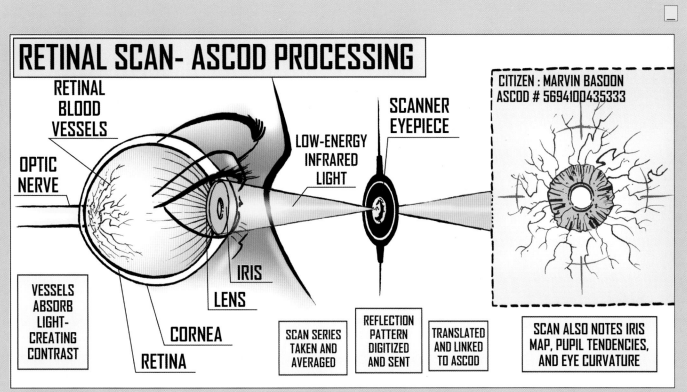

RETINAL SCAN- ASCOD PROCESSING

RETINAL BLOOD VESSELS

OPTIC NERVE

LOW-ENERGY INFRARED LIGHT

SCANNER EYEPIECE

CITIZEN : MARVIN BASDON
ASCOD # 5694100435333

IRIS

LENS

CORNEA

RETINA

VESSELS ABSORB LIGHT- CREATING CONTRAST

SCAN SERIES TAKEN AND AVERAGED

REFLECTION PATTERN DIGITIZED AND SENT

TRANSLATED AND LINKED TO ASCOD

SCAN ALSO NOTES IRIS MAP, PUPIL TENDENCIES, AND EYE CURVATURE

ACSOD is encoded via citizen biometrics, including retinal scans. For eyeless citizens, a nano chip is implanted.

Diagram Credit: L. Roberts

Temporary Labor Assignment (TLA) [edit]

When Terrans made the choice to emigrate to Mars during the Meltdown, more often than not, they escaped extremely dire situations in their home regions, including war, drought, and famine. In deciding to take the radical step of emigrating, these humans took action to assure the future for their families. But they were in many cases without resources, unable to pay for their passage, nor the substantial costs of setting up a Homestead to begin hygrofarming or algae tanking.

Arex's founder, Tac Nontilor, foresaw this problem when he first proposed the Homestead program. His revolutionary solution was to allow these first-wave Homesteaders to pay for their passage and equipment by becoming better Martian citizens, and contributing a portion of their labor, or the fruits of their labor, to developing Mars. He called these contracts Civic Labor Agreements. The labor of early settlers had a major impact on the human habitability of Mars.

Opponents of the practice misleadingly took to calling the Civic Laborers, "Indents," after the indenturement contracts enforced during the brutal colonizations by European Terrans of various Terran landmasses such as those later known as Australia and the United States of America (see article on Pre-Meltdown Geopolitical Boundaries and Nation-States).

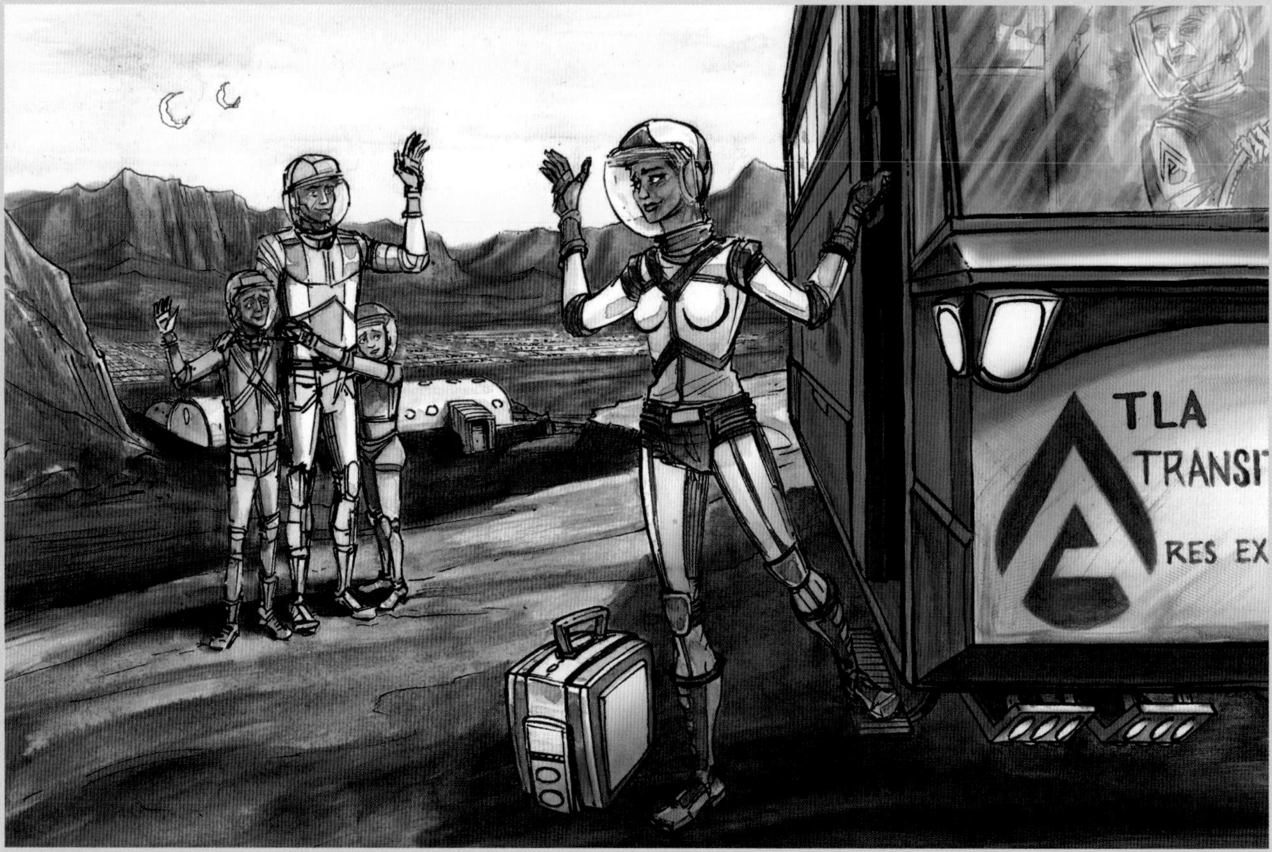
TLA
TRANSI
RES EX

A Civic Laborer boards transport to her Temporary Labor Assignment. Photo Credit: L. Roberts

Unfortunately, due to unexpectedly adverse conditions, many Civic Laborers overreached their ability to produce sufficient quantities of water or whatever other agricultural products they had agreed to contribute, and Arex (Then known as Ares Exploration Company) was left with a difficult dilemma: how to maintain fairness among settlers, yet support the growth of the colony. Thus was born a revolutionary concept: the Temporary Labor Assignment (TLA). The TLA, though involuntary in the sense that implementation would be triggered based on the status of an individual or family's ACSOD, proved an extremely efficient vehicle both to develop new resources for the planet (in particular via asteroid mining) as well as to erase large amounts of family debt, as Arex pays generous hazard bonuses for off-world assignments, and decease in the service of a TLA triggers automatic full debt forgiveness for the immediate family members (up to 4 individuals) of the defunct worker.

Asteroid Mining [edit]

Early attempts at asteroid mining involved altering asteroids' orbits until they could be captured into Near Earth Orbit. This approach has obvious dangers, but the increasingly dire environmental conditions coming to bear on Earth during the 2040s made exporting mining activities off world too attractive to resist. The first two asteroids captured (2007AJAM8 and 2010JRMA6) provided much-needed rocket fuel used by Ares Exploration Company (later Arex) for its initial colonization forays to Mars with the Pioneers, and the gold and platinum mined was so plentiful that it caused a short-lived global economic panic in 2047 as the price of gold fell precipitously, and many of the forebears of those who later became Third Wave Martian settlers, popularly known as Freemen, lost the majority of their wealth. This incident is memorialized in the lore of the Freemen as the End of the Yellow Brick Road and marks the beginning of their fixation as a group on "Blue," or water. (See article on Freemen (Martian Survivalist Colonies)).

Asteroid 2023QVC6, AKA "Black Sky"

Photo Credit: L. Roberts

The third asteroid being dragged into Earth orbit, 2023QVC6, popularly known as, "Black Sky," missed its target and collided with Earth near Boca Raton, United States of America, on 2052. The resulting destruction was massive, with an estimated 65,000 immediate casualties, and another 86,000 over the next few months. Ironically, this terrible disaster may have postponed the demise of the rest of Florida (see article on Pre-Meltdown Geographical Land Masses) for a bit longer, as the dust in the atmosphere postponed the Meltdown by an estimated 5 years.

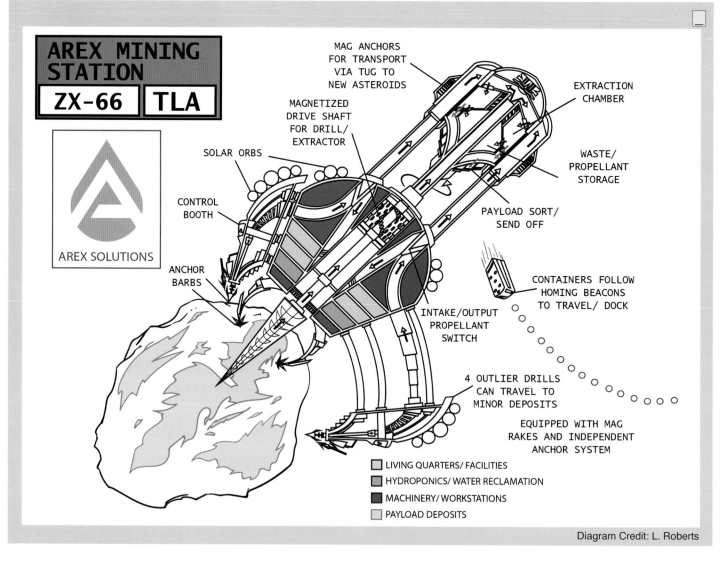

AREX MINING STATION
ZX-66 **TLA**

AREX SOLUTIONS

MAG ANCHORS FOR TRANSPORT VIA TUG TO NEW ASTEROIDS

MAGNETIZED DRIVE SHAFT FOR DRILL/ EXTRACTOR

EXTRACTION CHAMBER

SOLAR ORBS

WASTE/ PROPELLANT STORAGE

CONTROL BOOTH

PAYLOAD SORT/ SEND OFF

ANCHOR BARBS

CONTAINERS FOLLOW HOMING BEACONS TO TRAVEL/ DOCK

INTAKE/OUTPUT PROPELLANT SWITCH

4 OUTLIER DRILLS CAN TRAVEL TO MINOR DEPOSITS

EQUIPPED WITH MAG RAKES AND INDEPENDENT ANCHOR SYSTEM

LIVING QUARTERS/ FACILITIES
HYDROPONICS/ WATER RECLAMATION
MACHINERY/ WORKSTATIONS
PAYLOAD DEPOSITS

Diagram Credit: L. Roberts

After the Black Sky disaster, asteroid mining companies abandoned the near-Earth-orbit strategy and began mining asteroids more or less in situ. (Although two large icy asteroids were intentionally crashed into Mars in 2054 and 2057 to generate atmosphere, heat, and humidity as part of a terraformation stage later criticized as "extreme" and "dangerous." (See article on Mars Terraformation Strategies.) As a result of the more-dangerous deep space work conditions, however, the Worker Failure rate went up, and incidences of SPTSD (Space Post-Traumatic Stress Disorder) were on the rise, which raised the mining companies' insurance premiums to the point where many of these companies were faced with bankruptcy. Fortunately, this rise in Worker Failure coincided with an influx of available workers due to the inception of the TLA system on Mars, which stabilized worker population. Asteroid mining is today the main source of processed ore for all Human colonies as well as Terra, where mining has been completely outlawed since 2085. It also plays a crucial role in providing water to Mars during the ongoing sequera[1]. While space labor remains dangerous, particularly in Asteroid Belt and Kuiper Belt assignments, annual casualty rates have come down quite a bit in recent years [needs citation], in contrast to the early history of asteroid mining.

[1]Sequera: severe drought conditions that show signs of having become baseline expectations. See articles on Mars Meteorological Conditions, Equatorial Earth post-Meltdown Sequera.

Ismail Khan [edit]

Ismail Khan was a water prospector, pilot, and engineer who arrived on Mars in 2073 (11ME) early in the second wave of settlements. Handsome and charismatic, he was also an early reality-vidblast star on the popular Pioneers series, seasons 4-13.

As an employee of Arex, Khan, in conjunction with his partner, Nadia Vodyanova, developed the first prototype hydrosails today used by moisture farmers across Mars.

During the period 2075-2079 (13-14ME) Khan and Vodyanova prospected for water extensively in Vastitis. They discovered several important water sources that have since run dry due to over-utilization, or to some other unknown factor [needs citation].

During their last trip together, Aprilbis 11 of 14ME, Vodyanova reported that she had detected elevated levels of humidity in a cavern in Mawrth Vallis [needs citation]. She and Khan entered the cavern, and saw what she described as "tracks" in the dust, at which point she proposed leaving the cavern. Khan demurred, and descended deeper into the cavern. He was not seen again.

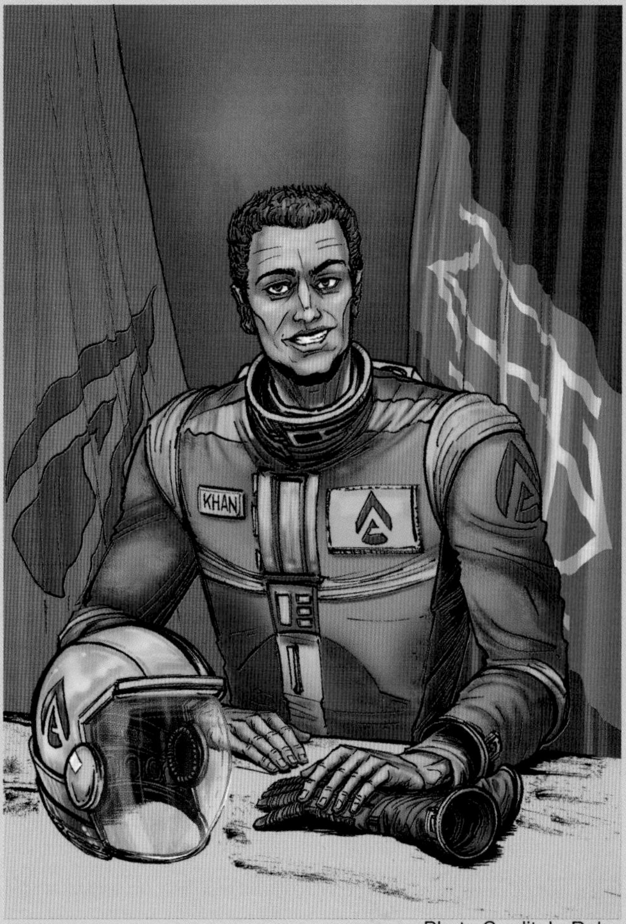
KHAN

Photo Credit: L. Roberts

Commander Ismail Khan in 2072.

Vodyanova contended that he was abducted by indigenous Martians, a suggestion for which she was ridiculed until her death in 48ME. Sightings of what appear to be some kind of native species of Martian [needs citation] in the last 11 years have rehabilitated her reputation to an extent.

A recent run of the popular retro "comic strip" *Tales of the Early Colonists* contains several factual inaccuracies.

- Ismail Khan and Nadia Vodyanova wore full pressure suits when taking surface walks.
- Third Wave settlers known as the Freemen did not arrive on Mars until 2090 (20ME), and have never been documented as having engaged in open firefights with other settlers.
- Cyrus Khan, nephew of Ismail Khan, and later the founder of the controversial New Order of Green Men, was never taken along on water prospecting or hydro-drilling missions. At the time of Ismail Khan's disappearance, he was four years old.

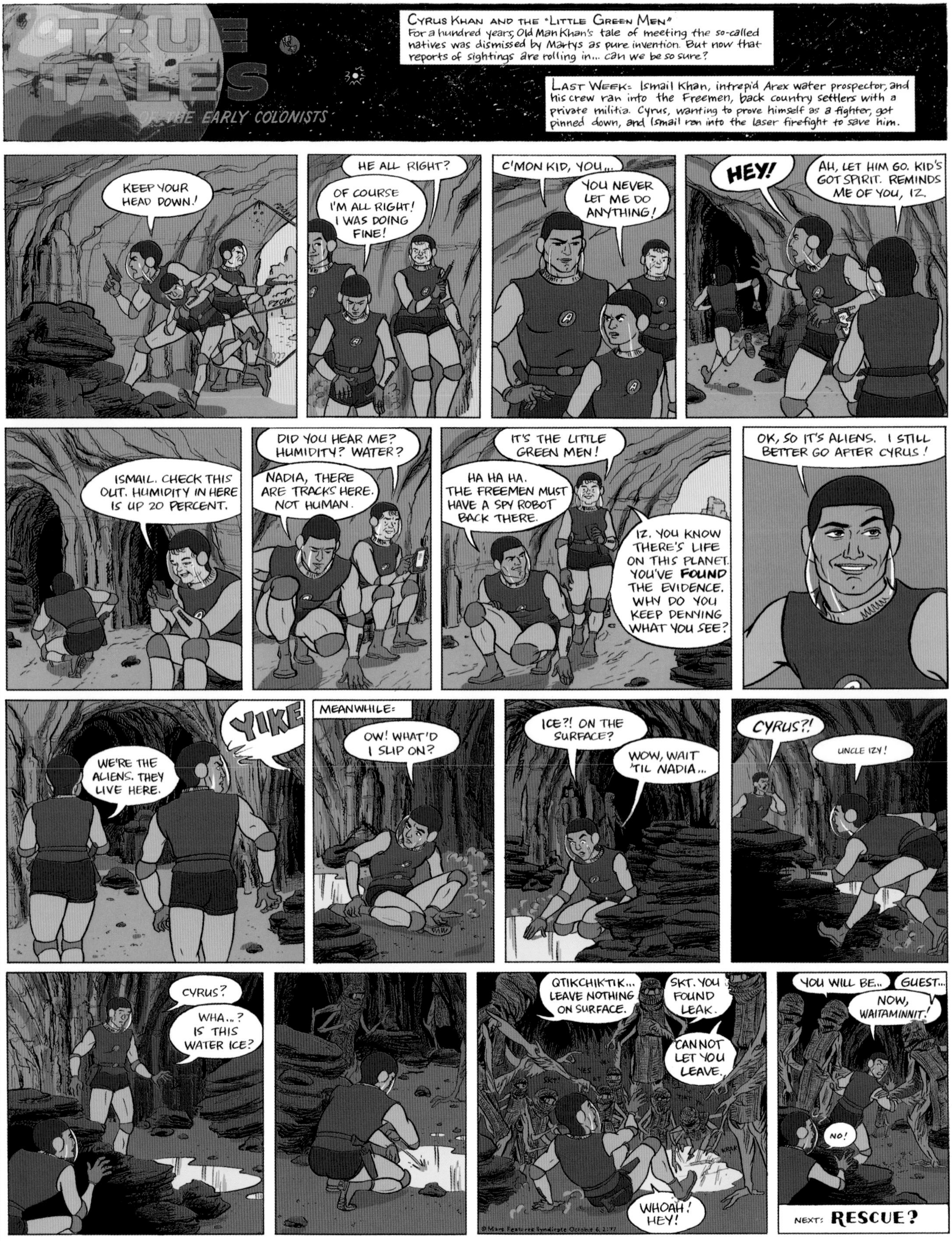

TRUE TALES OF THE EARLY COLONISTS
CYRUS KHAN AND THE "LITTLE GREEN MEN"
For a hundred years, Old Man Khan's tale of meeting the so-called natives was dismissed by Martys as pure invention. But now that reports of sightings are rolling in... can we be so sure?
LAST WEEK: Ismail Khan, intrepid Arex water prospector, and his crew ran into the Freemen, back country settlers with a private militia. Cyrus, wanting to prove himself as a fighter, got pinned down, and Ismail ran into the laser firefight to save him.
KEEP YOUR HEAD DOWN!
FZOW!
HE ALL RIGHT?
OF COURSE I'M ALL RIGHT! I WAS DOING FINE!
C'MON KID, YOU...
YOU NEVER LET ME DO ANYTHING!
HEY!
AH, LET HIM GO. KID'S GOT SPIRIT. REMINDS ME OF YOU, IZ.
ISMAIL. CHECK THIS OUT. HUMIDITY IN HERE IS UP 20 PERCENT.
DID YOU HEAR ME? HUMIDITY? WATER?
NADIA, THERE ARE TRACKS HERE. NOT HUMAN.
IT'S THE LITTLE GREEN MEN!
HA HA HA. THE FREEMEN MUST HAVE A SPY ROBOT BACK THERE.
IZ. YOU KNOW THERE'S LIFE ON THIS PLANET. YOU'VE FOUND THE EVIDENCE. WHY DO YOU KEEP DENYING WHAT YOU SEE?
OK, SO IT'S ALIENS. I STILL BETTER GO AFTER CYRUS!
YIKE
WE'RE THE ALIENS. THEY LIVE HERE.
MEANWHILE:
OW! WHAT'D I SLIP ON?
ICE?! ON THE SURFACE?
WOW, WAIT 'TIL NADIA...
CYRUS?!
UNCLE IZY!
CYRUS?
WHA...? IS THIS WATER ICE?
QTIKCHIKTIK... LEAVE NOTHING ON SURFACE.
SKT. YOU FOUND LEAK.
CAN NOT LET YOU LEAVE.
WHOAH! HEY!
© Mars Features Syndicate Octobis 6, 2177
YOU WILL BE...
GUEST...
NOW, WAITAMINNIT!
NO!
NEXT: RESCUE?

Mars Features Syndicate Octobis 6 2177.

Photo Credit: J. Abel

Timeline of Mars Colonization [edit]

2050-2055 (0 - 2ME) The first wave of Martian settlers, known now as the "Pioneers" due to the reality vidblast series of the same name that documented the period and funded 78.95% [2] of the cost of the journey, arrived on Mars. The Pioneers arrived in a series of 9 ships owned by Ares Exploratory Corporation (later Arex) with international cooperation. Co-sponsoring nations included United States of America, the Russian Union, the European Alliance, Ghana, China, Japan, Indiastan, and United South American States, along with either 23 or 36 other countries and corporate units (up to 13 contributors remain in dispute, despite 17 cases brought and settled at the International Space Court).

The Pioneers were chosen in a very public sorting on the basis of their training and abilities, alongside personality traits and lack of immediate family members. Despite this process, attrition rate was high, due to accident, self-inflicted injury, as well as disease, as medicine had not yet developed Genetic Print technology. There were also a total of 20 seats reserved on the ships for private passengers who paid their own way.

2055-2070 (2 - 10ME) First generation Martians born, more ships arrived. Human population rises to 1000. Terraformation efforts managed to create a minimal atmosphere, and build a small amount of organic material in (carefully isolated) soil.

2060 (5ME) Bombardment with asteroids added water to atmosphere, and also resulted in the deaths of up to 236 Martians.

2065 (7ME) Arex built space elevators on Earth and Mars.

2072 (11ME) The Homestead program began shipping large numbers of settlers to Mars. Initially, many settlers self-funded the trip, or were sponsored by governments, but once the Hot War began (2076-2081) the majority of the settlers arrived under indenturement contracts with Arex. The Homestead program spanned the years 2072 - 2110 (30ME), peaking in 2087. Approximately 123,784 human settlers arrived on Mars in this program, largely from the equatorial region of Earth, the area most brutally affected by the Meltdown.

2075-85 (12 - 17ME) An unknown number of ships (estimated 7) carrying members of an extremist Prepper cult left their private Habitat-style orbitenvironment and arrived on Mars. It's thought that at least one ship was lost in transit, and that in the range of 1300 undocumented settlers arrived in this wave. These are the ancestors of the Martians now known as Freemen, who tend to live in large self-sufficient mobile habitats in the outback of Mars, protected from surveillance by satellite shielding and powerful armaments. Despite the fact that these settlements are illegal, the MarsGuard has thus far proven unequal to the task of eradicating them.

Martians known as Freemen are thought to live in large mobile habitats protected from surveillance by satellite shielding and powerful armaments. [Artist's Rendition]

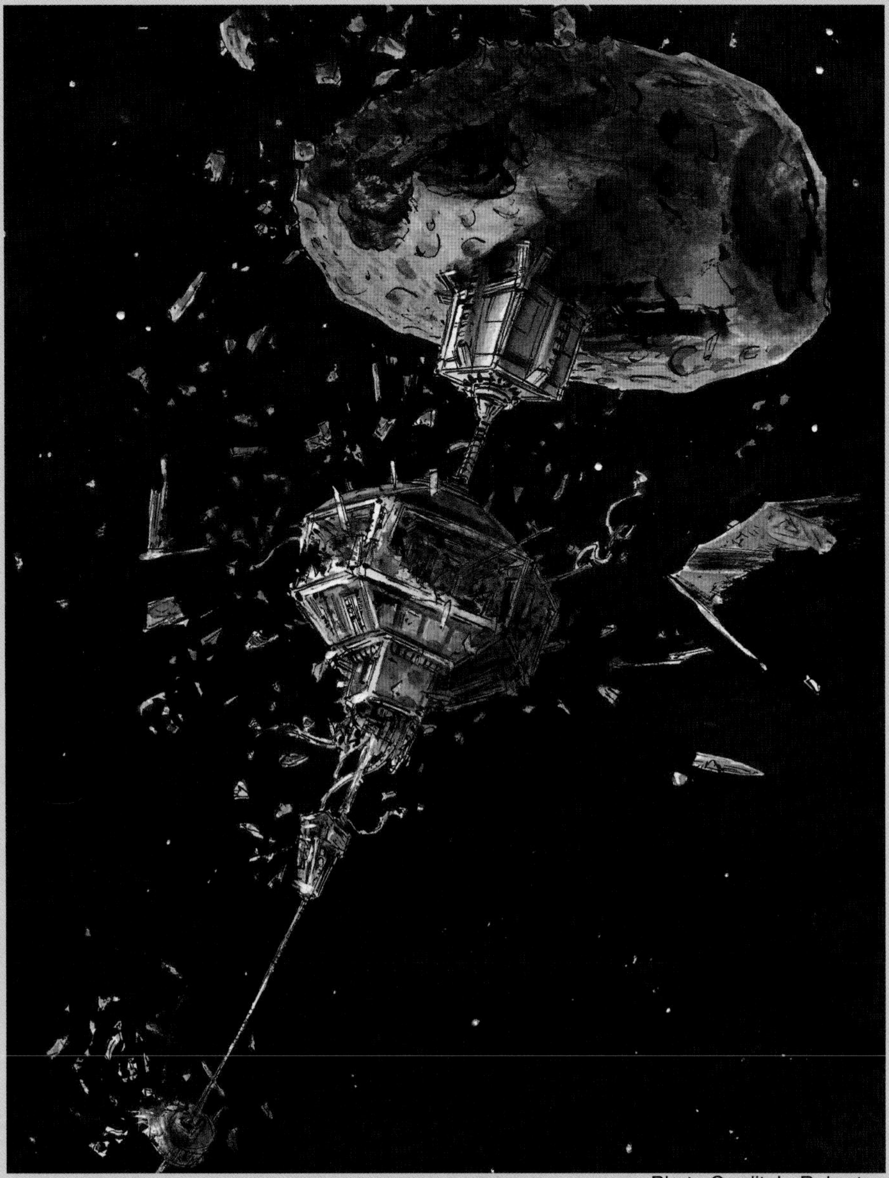

Photo Credit: L. Roberts

Martian partisan terrorists destroy the Homestead carrier Laura Ingalls Wilder in 2111 (30ME).

2080-82 (15 - 16ME) The Meltdown: Earth suffered catastrophic environmental collapse.

2083 (16ME) Earth ceased sending financial support to Mars. This year also marks Earth's complete ban on any kind of carbon-generating activity, creating a robust market for industrial and mining products from Mars and nearby asteroids.

2084 (17ME) Earth passed the Secure Our World Act (SOW), effectively banning any off-world settlers, whether originating on Mars, Europa, asteroids, or the orbiting Habitats, from returning to the surface.

2111 (30ME) The last of the Homestead ships arrived at the Martian space elevator, and was destroyed by Martian partisan terrorists before it could return to Earth, destroying 1.3 billion oras of cargo, killing three crew members, and causing massive damage to the space elevator itself. This is generally thought to mark the end of the Colonization phase of Martian history.